sight

First U.S. edition published 1985 by Barron's Educational Series, Inc.

© Parramón Ediciones, S.A., 1983

All inquiries should be addressed to:
Barron's Educational Series, Inc.
250 Wireless Boulevard
Hauppauge, New York 11788

International Standard Book No. 0-8120-3564-X

Library of Congress Catalog Card No. 84-28210

Library of Congress Cataloging in Publication Data

Parramón, José María
　　The fives senses—sight.

　　Translation of: Los cinco sentidos—la vista.
　　Summary: A short scientific explanation of our sense
of sight, with a diagram of the eye.
　　1. Vision—Juvenile literature. [1. Vision.
2. Eye　3. Senses and sensation]　I. Puig, J.J.
II. Rius, María, ill.　III. Title.
QP475.7.P3613　1985　　612'.84　　84-28210
ISBN 0-8120-3564-X

0 1 2 3　　0 9 8

Register Book Number: 785
Legal Deposit: B-6721-90

Printed in Spain by Emsa
Diputación, 116 - 08015 Barcelona

the five senses

sight

María Rius

J. M. Parramón   J. J. Puig

BARRON'S

New York • Toronto • Sydney

Look, look!
Look at all the things you can see.

See the fireworks shoot fast through the air…

...and see the little turtle going so very, very slowly.

See black squares and white squares.

Look at the rainbow. It fills the whole sky with colors.

Look at the puppy playing in the field...

...look at the tiny ant.

Look at the great big elephant!

Read books…look at the pictures.

See the moon.

See the sun.

Look, look! There's a clock on the bell tower.

Look at television.

Everything that you see, you see with your EYES.

SIGHT

Our senses are the way we find out about the world we live in. We see with our eyes, and that tells us about things that are outside of our bodies. Our eyes give us pictures of the way things look.

You can see to read with your eyes, or tell where you're going. You can play ball games, or find your friends. Your eyes show you light, color, shape, and size. Your eyes can even help you figure out how far away something is.

Parts of the Eye

There are many parts to your eye, and each one of them helps you to see. The light goes in through an opening called the *pupil.* That's the black dot in the center of your eye. The *iris,* or colored part around the pupil, can change the size of the opening. This lets in more or less light. The *lens* focuses the light rays as they shine on the *retina;* the *cornea* protects the lens. The *optic nerve* carries the picture from the retina to your brain.

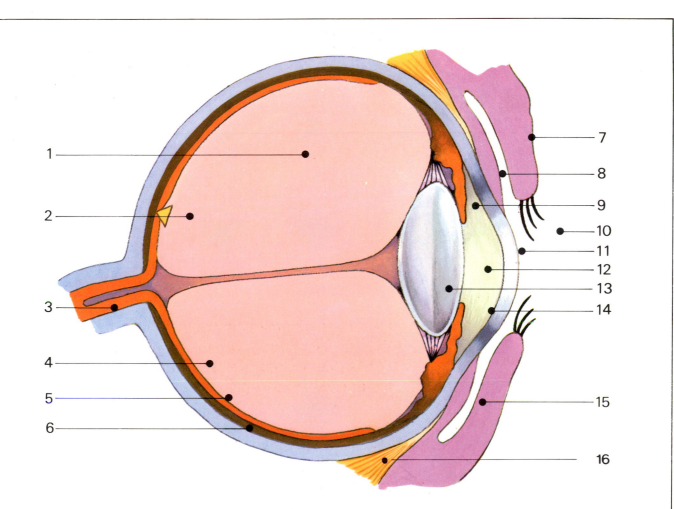

THE EYE

1 Vitreous fluid	7 Top lid	12 Pupil
2 Rods and cones	8 Conjunctiva	13 Lens
3 Optic nerve	9 Iris	14 Aqueous fluid
4 Retina	10 Eyelashes	15 Lower lid
5 Choroid layer	11 Cornea	16 Eye muscle
6 Sclera		

SIGHT

When you look at your eyes in the mirror, you're only seeing a part of them. The whole eye is shaped like a round ball. But most of it is inside your head and protected by your skull. Only a small part is visible. Your *eyelids* and *eyelashes* protect your eyes, too. Your eyelids make it possible for you to close your eyes. That way, you can shut out the light when you are tired of looking at all the wonderful things there are to see. Closing your eyes makes it easier for you to go to sleep.

How Your Eye Works

Your eye is almost like a camera. Here's how it works. The light bouncing off the thing you are looking at goes into your eye through the pupil. As the light crosses your lens, the image gets focused—and also turned upside down! This image shines on the back of your eye, on the part called the *retina*. The *rods* and *cones* that line the retina help you see colors and the sharp details of what you're looking at. The optic nerve then carries the message to your brain.

The first thing your brain does is turn the picture right side up again. Then your brain figures out what it is seeing. Your brain also figures out what you should do about it. For example, if your eye sends a message to your brain that a ball is rolling right up to you, your brain figures out what you should do about it—catch it, of course.

Tears keep your eyes nice and wet and clean. When you blink, you clean out dust and anything else that might make your eye feel uncomfortable. You blink about twenty times a minute.

Your *eye muscles* make it possible for you to move your eyes all around without moving your head. You can look up or down, or left or right. You can move your eyes along a line of words, and then back again to the beginning of the next line.

Sometimes people have trouble seeing things. When they have trouble seeing things that are close but can see things far away easily, they are called *far-sighted.* When the opposite happens, and they can't see things that are far away but can see things that are near, they are called *near-sighted.* Wearing glasses helps correct seeing problems.

You should always take good care of your eyes. Look around you at all the wonderful things there are for you to see with them.

S'MORE PLATE TECTONICS

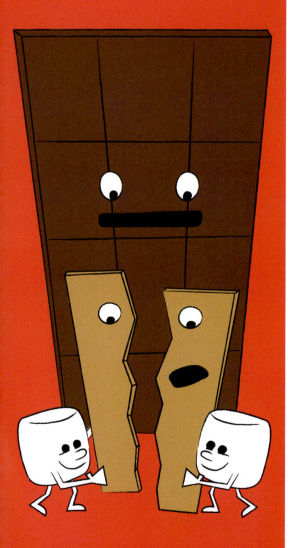

HAVE YOU ever noticed that Earth's continents fit together like a jigsaw puzzle? That's because Earth's crust (outer shell) is made of about 30 pieces called *plates*. Over millions of years, the plates move around quite a bit. The plates "float" on Earth's *mantle*, a layer of hot rock beneath the crust. Some plates spread apart, while others crash into one another or sink into the mantle.

The idea that describes how the plates move is called *plate tectonics*. This idea explains many features of Earth's surface. It also explains why volcanoes and earthquakes often occur in certain places.

Earth's plates only move a few inches or centimeters a year, so plate tectonics is a little hard to observe in action. Fortunately, you can make a quick-moving model of Earth's plate tectonics with the same ingredients you'd use to make a s'more.

MATERIALS

- Microwave
- Glass baking pan or loaf pan (microwave safe)
- Bag of mini-marshmallows
- Chocolate bar (or two)
- Graham crackers
- Camera
- Potholders

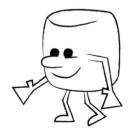

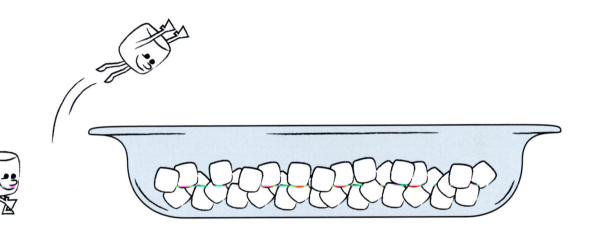

Create the ASTHENOSPHERE

The *asthenosphere* is part of Earth's *mantle*, which lies beneath the planet's solid crust. Like the rest of the mantle, the asthenosphere is made of rock. But this rock isn't like the solid rocks you pick up on the surface. Deep inside our planet, temperatures reach thousands of degrees, and the weight of all the rock above presses down with great pressure. This tremendous heat and pressure melts and squishes the asthenosphere's rock so that it behaves less like a rigid solid and more like a marshmallow.

Spread a layer of mini-marshmallows across the bottom of the glass pan. This layer will be your asthenosphere. The marshmallow layer doesn't have to be very deep, and it's okay if it's a little uneven. The real asthenosphere is uneven too.

Create the LITHOSPHERE

The *lithosphere* is the name for Earth's tectonic plates. These plates float on top of the asthenosphere.

The lithosphere actually has two parts. The top part is the solid crust that you live on. You'll use graham crackers to represent Earth's crust. The other part of the lithosphere is part of the mantle, right below the crust and above the asthenosphere. This layer of mantle is denser than the marshmallowlike asthenosphere. But it's more "melty" than the solid crust. You'll use chocolate for this lower layer of the lithosphere.

Break the graham crackers and chocolate bar into pieces. Place the chocolate pieces on the marshmallows first. Then place the graham cracker pieces on top of the chocolate pieces. Remember, each "plate" should consist of a layer of chocolate (mantle) *and* a layer of crust (graham cracker.)

You can make your plates different shapes and sizes, just like Earth's continents. Leave some plates close together. But make sure you separate some pieces by large gaps, so the marshmallows show through. There are gaps between the tectonic plates on Earth, too—and interesting things happen at these gaps.

Finally, take a picture of your "world map." You'll want to compare the positions of your graham-cracker-and-chocolate tectonic plates now and afterwards.

HEAT *things up*

You've made a working model of Earth's lithosphere and asthenosphere. But there's something important missing from this picture—the great heat and pressure beneath the Earth's surface! That's where the microwave comes in.

Ask an adult to help you microwave the pan for 10 seconds at a time. Using potholders, take the pan out of the microwave, and take a new picture. Have your tectonic plates changed their positions?

Microwave the pan again for 10 seconds, and take another picture, then repeat, and repeat again, and so on. Do not microwave the pan for more than 10 seconds at a time. And always watch the pan closely to make sure the marshmallows don't puff over the edge or burn!

What happens to the graham cracker crust when things get hot? After about 30 seconds, the marshmallows should start to puff up. After about 60 seconds, the chocolate layer of the lithosphere should start melting. After 90 seconds or so, some of your graham crackers may even start sinking into your asthenosphere. After 120 seconds, let your experiment rest.

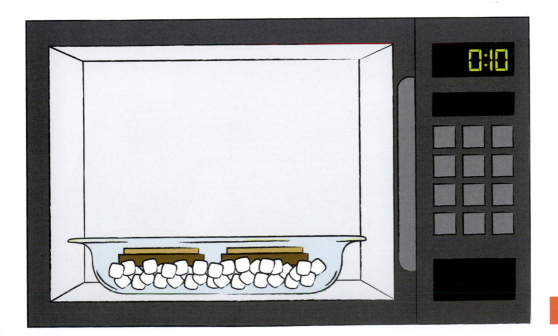

Observe your plates' **MOTION**

Let your lithosphere and asthenosphere cool completely and take a final picture. By now, the melted chocolate should have resolidified, and the marshmallows may even have formed a hard crust.

Compare the series of pictures you took. How did the hot marshmallows cause your tectonic plates to move? If your graham crackers were flat, are they sloped like mountains now? Did you notice anything happen near the gaps between your plates? Melted chocolate and marshmallows may have spewed up between those gaps.

On Earth, the boundaries between plates are dangerous places. Earthquakes often occur near *faults*, where two plates touch and scrape against each other. Your graham crackers don't weigh very much, but Earth's plates weigh a lot. Imagine you are a tiny person living on top of one of those graham crackers. Even a relatively tiny shift or scrape can be destructive.

Volcanoes also occur near gaps in the crust, where *magma*—molten rock from the mantle—can easily flow up to the surface. When the magma reaches the surface, it is called *lava*. The lava cools and becomes solid, and over time it builds up mountains, or volcanoes.

REPEAT *the experiment*

Clean the glass pan (hot tap water works well to dissolve sticky marshmallow) and repeat the experiment with a different pattern of tectonic plates. (If you'd rather not sacrifice another chocolate bar in the name of science, feel free to leave it out—the activity works fine with just marshmallows and graham crackers.) Take pictures and compare the motions of the differently shaped plates. What patterns do you observe?

VOLCANO ERUPTION

VOLCANOES are one of the most exciting—and dangerous—natural events on Earth! Hot, molten rock spews up from deep beneath the ground, shoots into the air, and spills onto the land below as lava flows. Some volcanoes may release massive clouds of sizzling ash, cause fires, and trigger landslides or avalanches that can create much damage.

In this activity, you will construct your own volcano. Then you'll set off a chemical reaction that will cause it to erupt!

MATERIALS

- Small jar (no lid necessary)
- Newspaper
- Tray
- Modeling clay
- Twigs, grass, moss, or rocks (for decoration)
- Water
- Food coloring (optional)
- Liquid dish soap
- Baking soda
- Measuring spoons
- Measuring cup (with spout for easy pouring)
- Distilled white vinegar

BUILD *your volcano*

Picture a volcano. You might imagine a tall mountain with steep sides. Actually, there are many different types of volcanoes. They come in all shapes and sizes. Here, you will build a *shield volcano*. The word *shield* refers to the volcano's shape. It looks like the gentle curve of a warrior's shield.

Volcanoes tend to make messes when they erupt. Spread plenty of newspaper on a table or the floor before you begin. (You can also build your volcano outside.) Place a tray in the center of the newspapers. Then place the jar in the middle of the tray. Use modeling clay to build your volcano around the jar. (Remember, a shield volcano is a wide shape with a gentle curve at the top.) Make sure you don't cover the opening of the jar.

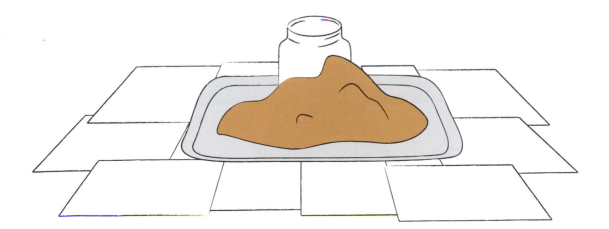

Lava is very hot!

Lava from a volcanic eruption can be up to 12 times hotter than boiling water. That's 1200°C (2544°F)!

Watch the ERUPTION

Eruptions happen when magma reaches Earth's surface. The magma chamber breaks open when the pressure inside it becomes too high. As soon as the magma hits the air, it's called *lava*.

To turn your magma into lava, carefully pour the vinegar into the jar. When the vinegar touches the baking soda, a chemical reaction will occur. The reaction produces gas that will cause the lava to rise. The dish soap makes the lava extra foamy.

Your eruption will happen very quickly, so pay close attention! How long does it last? How much lava did it create? Record your observations as you go.

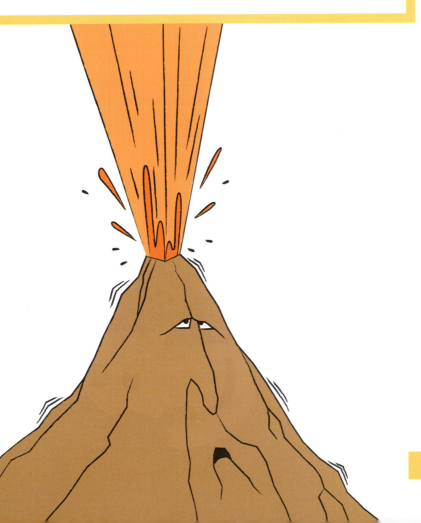

FINDING AXEL

"I wonder if my grandfather, Doc U. Ment, ever tried the same experiments that I've been performing when he was studying science."

Mollie rushed over to the wall-length bookcase filled with Grandfather Doc U. Ment's reference books. She searched the shelves.

"Here's his Experiment Log! He told me that he wrote notes, observations, and conclusions about all of his experiences! Let's see..."

She pulled the book off the shelf, its worn cover almost torn off of the binding. As she paged through Grandfather's log, the bookshelf started to wobble and move. Pictures on the wall jiggled. Feline hid under the table. Mollie's legs started to shake as the room rumbled.

"What's happening? Is this a real earthquake? I feel like I'm spinning and gravity is all upside down!"

Mollie turned and saw the bookshelf slide across the wall, revealing a door to a secret room!

"What's this?"

Mollie peeked her head through the new doorway and saw…a hidden laboratory! There were strange objects everywhere—a solar system mobile hanging from the ceiling, colorful plants wildly growing, and even a large balloon trapped inside of a bottle! In the center of the room stood a rounded copper structure. Mollie rushed over to examine this curious contraption.

"A ROBOT!" Mollie said with excitement. "WOW! I have read about robots my entire life, like the ones in outer space or in factories, but I've never met one in person! I wonder who built this."

Next to the robot lay a manual titled, **Axel the Robot: Doc U. Ment's Master Project Manual.**

"Axel? So that's your name. You are my grandfather's work! It's amazing! I'm sure that Grandfather meant for me to find his secret lab and this robot. But, wait," Mollie tapped Axel on the chest. "Axel isn't working. Oh, I know! I will reboot him! It will be the perfect test of my scientific knowledge."

Mollie opened the instruction manual and began reading.

"Wow. I'll have to try all types of activities to get this right!"

CREATE ARTIFICIAL GRAVITY

WHAT IS GRAVITY? Scientists are still trying to figure out the precise answer to that question. But one thing they do know is that gravity acts as a *force*—that is, a push or a pull. Massive objects, like planets, have a lot of gravity. When you jump, you don't go flying into outer space because Earth's gravity pulls you back down to the ground. So if a bucket full of water is upside-down, you'd think that Earth's gravity would pull the water out of the bucket—in other words, that the water would fall and splash all over the place.

But gravity isn't the only force working. Spinning objects have forces too. When you spin around fast on a merry-go-round, you may feel like you're about to be flung off the side. That feeling you experience is called a *centrifugal force*. If you hang on to the rail of the merry-go-round, the force seems to push you sideways against the rail. (It also might make you dizzy.)

This same spinning force, in certain circumstances, can "push" sideways harder than Earth's gravity can "pull" down. It can even act as a kind of artificial gravity—and keep water in an upside-down bucket from falling out! Go ahead and try it!

Make sure to do this experiment outside in an open space without people or other valuable objects nearby. If your artificial gravity doesn't work quite right, you're going to get wet!

MATERIALS

- A plastic bucket with a handle
- Small toys, balls, or other solid objects
- Water
- A rope or bungee cord

PREPARE *the bucket*

In order to create artificial gravity, you need to be able to spin the bucket around in a wide, steady circle. Loop the rope or cord around the bucket's handle. Tie a knot. Then, grasping the rope or cord, try swinging the bucket around vertically, like you're winding up a softball pitch. Be sure you do this in an open space, without any people or valuable objects nearby.

You may need to adjust the length of the rope so that the bucket doesn't hit the ground as it swings. And if your bucket has a big handle—or if you have long arms—you may not need the rope or cord at all. (Careful not to spin it too fast, or you might lose control.)

Test your ARTIFICIAL GRAVITY

Place a few unbreakable toys or other small solid objects inside the bucket. (You can use a baseball, a spoon, an action figure—anything small that you wouldn't mind dropping.)

You'd think these objects would fall out of the bucket if the bucket is upside-down, right? Try swinging the bucket around in a steady circle. Do the objects fall out? Or do they cling to the bottom of the bucket, even when the bucket is upside-down? How fast do you need to spin the bucket to get the objects to stay put?

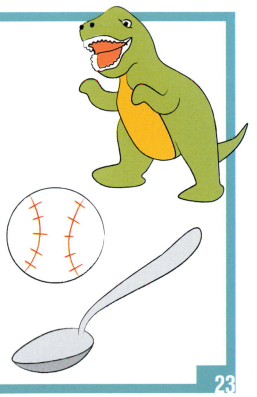

23

DEFY GRAVITY *with water*

Fill the bucket up with water about halfway. (If it's too heavy for you to lift, just use less water.) Then, carefully, start swinging the bucket around, as you've practiced. What happens to the water while the bucket is spinning? What happens to the water if the bucket suddenly *stops* spinning? And can you manage to stop spinning the bucket without splashing yourself?

REAL-LIFE ROBOTS: Robots in Outer Space

If humans ever live in an outer space colony, it might have the same kind of artificial gravity as your bucket. In the 1970's, the National Aeronautics and Space Administration (NASA) came up with a space colony design that's shaped like a torus—a donut, in other words. The torus colony spins around and around. People live in a hollow space inside. Just like objects and water in your bucket, people on the spinning colony would be flung against the donut's interior. "Down" would feel like the outer edge of the donut, while "up" would feel like the hole in the center.

NASA has no plans to build a space colony anytime soon, but they'd probably need robots to do it. In fact, robotic machines helped build and maintain the International Space Station that's floating above Earth right now. This station doesn't have artificial gravity, but it has plenty of robotic devices. For example, a remote-controlled robotic arm called Canadarm2, seen here, can "carry" astronauts on spacewalks.

TORNADO IN A BOTTLE

TORNADOES are some of the most violent storms. Some tornado winds can swirl at speeds up to 300 miles (480 kilometers) per hour. Such winds are strong enough to lift a house from its foundation! The most damaging tornadoes occur in powerful thunderstorms called *supercells*. Because tornadoes are so dangerous, scientists have to be careful when studying how supercells develop.

A supercell storm may form when warm, moist air near the ground starts quickly spiraling upward. If you've ever seen a hot air balloon, you've seen how warm air has a tendency to rise. Warm air rises because it is less dense, or lighter, than cold air. So if there's a big layer of warm air stuck underneath a high layer of cold air, the situation is unstable. The low layer of warm air wants to rise, like a balloon, and the high cold air wants to fall.

But, a low-lying layer of warm air is not enough to create a supercell storm or a tornado. You also need wind. When winds blow at different speeds or directions at different heights in the sky, they may cause the warm air to twist as it rises up. This twisting motion forms a *vortex*. A supercell is a giant vortex of stormclouds. A tornado occurs when a supercell vortex touches the ground.

Now it's time to make a vortex of your own. Luckily, this vortex won't be quite as powerful as a real tornado!

MATERIALS

- 2 large, clear plastic soft-drink bottles with screw-top lids
- Strong waterproof glue
- Water
- Hole punch
- Confetti, glitter, or other small bits of paper

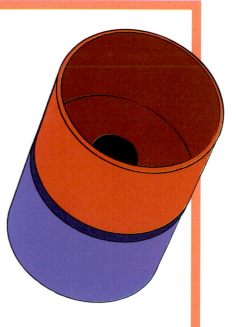

Construct your **VORTEX CONNECTOR**

Remove the screw-top lid from the two soft-drink bottles. Glue the tops of the two lids together. Ask an adult to help you punch a hole the size of a drinking straw through the middle of the lids.

This double-lid will connect your two bottles. Water from one bottle will drain through the double-lid and into the other bottle. If you're not feeling particularly crafty, you can purchase a pre-made plastic connector at many craft stores instead of making your own double-lid.

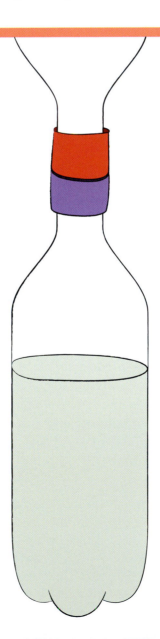

ARRANGE *your "air" layers*

Fill one of the bottles about three-fourths full of water. Screw on the lid connector. Then screw the empty bottle on top. Make sure that the lid connector is screwed on tightly to each bottle and the seal is waterproof. And, just to be safe, perform the rest of the experiment outside or over a sink, in case anything does splash.

Scientists use unmanned aerial vehicles (UAV's) to study supercell storms and tornadoes. Also called drones, UAV's are remotely piloted, so scientists use them to fly into dangerous weather that might harm a human pilot.

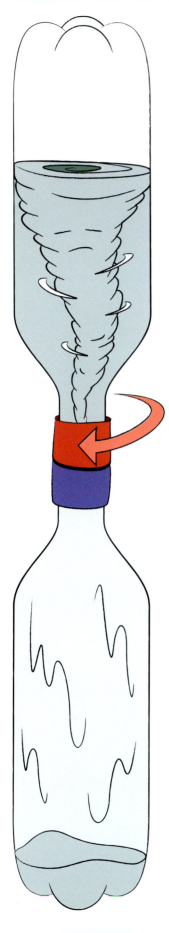

Form a VORTEX

Turn the bottles over so that the one with water is on top. Hold the bottles still. Watch what happens closely. The water should drain completely from the top bottle into the lower bottle, like sand in an hourglass. As the top bottle's water drains, the lower bottle's air rises up to fill the space.

Now turn the bottles over again, only this time, spin the bottles. What happens now? The water on top should form a vortex—and it should drain into the lower bottle much, much faster.

What's going on? Remember that a tornado needs two layers of air to form—a warm layer on bottom and a cold layer on top. This arrangement is unstable! It's the reverse of the natural order of things—because warm air is less dense, it wants to be on the top, while denser cold air wants to be on the bottom.

In your bottle, the water acts like the layer of cold air. Like cold air, water is dense, or heavy, so it falls, while the air in the empty bottle is less dense than water, and so it rises. So when you put the water-filled bottle on top of the air-filled bottle, you've created an unstable—and tornado-friendly—condition.

But remember, a tornado also needs another condition to form—the storm has to be spinning. That's where your vortex comes in. You should be able to see how a vortex speeds everything up. When the bottles are spinning, the water drains faster, and the air rises faster. This extra speed is what gives tornadoes their destructive power.

Add DEBRIS

Let the water flow into one bottle. Then, unscrew the bottles from each other. Add bits of paper or glitter into the bottle with the water. Reconnect the two bottles and try the activity again. Can you see the tornado more clearly now?

Real tornadoes often look like dark funnels. That dark color actually comes from dust and dirt and other debris that the tornado winds have lifted up from the ground. Without this debris, a tornado would be as clear as air.

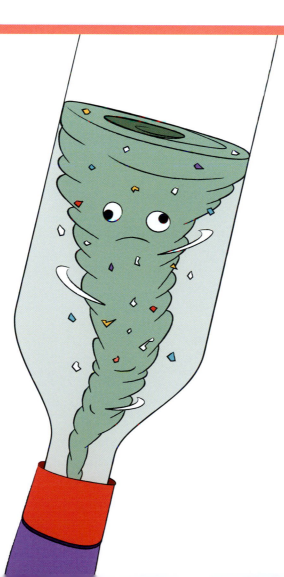

CREATE AN ANEMOMETER

YOU CAN SIMPLY measure the speeds of moving objects, such as a car or the wind, if you know the right method of measurement.

It's pretty easy to find how fast a car is going. First, you measure how far the car goes from point A to point B. Then, divide that distance by the time it takes to get there. The same goes for a bicycle, or a person walking.

The speed of the wind, on the other hand, is a little trickier to measure. Wind is moving air. But air isn't a solid like a car. It's a gas. You can't look at a piece of air and follow it on its journey like you can follow a car or a bike.

Fortunately, meteorologists (scientists who study weather) have learned how to measure the speed of the wind—and so can you! All you need is a weather instrument called an *anemometer*. Anemometers are usually placed outdoors so they can measure the speed of the wind as it whips by. Here's how to create your own anemometer!

MATERIALS

- 4 small paper cups
- 2 plastic drinking straws
- Stapler
- Tape
- Sturdy pencil with an eraser
- Thumbtack
- Marker or pen
- Timer or watch that measures seconds

ATTACH *the cups*

An anemometer is a bit like a windmill—the wind makes it spin. The four cups act like the blades of a windmill. The wind pushes against the inside of the cups, causing them to move in a circle—once you set them up properly, that is.

Ask an adult to help you staple two cups to the ends of each straw. First, lay the cups on their sides. The cups should open sideways, and should be facing *opposite* directions.

Then, position the straw lengthwise over the top of the two cups. The ends of the straw should almost reach the upper edge of each cup.

Once in position, carefully staple each end of the straw to the two cups. Remember, on each straw, the two cups should be facing *opposite* directions on either end. You should now have two cups connected to each straw. (Look at the pictures to help guide your work!)

ARRANGE *the cups*

Once the cups are connected to the straws, place the straws in an X-shape. The four cups should form a diamondlike shape. (Hint: If you draw an imaginary circle around the cups, the circle should pass through each cup's open end in turn.)

Tape the straws together where they cross, so that the X-shape locks in place. Make sure you tape the straws so that they form right angles.

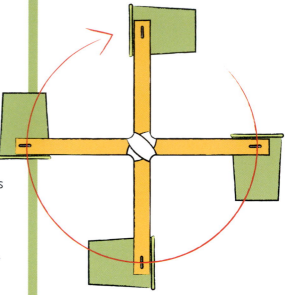

Balance your **ANEMOMETER**

Ask an adult to help you push the thumbtack through the taped straws where they cross. Be careful that you don't prick yourself! When you've pierced both straws, push the thumbtack into the center of the pencil's eraser.

Hold up the pencil, balancing the cups and straws on the pencil. You've just created an anemometer! It's okay if it wobbles a little—it just needs to hold all together.

Now, supply the wind by blowing on the cups. Do they spin around? (Hint: If you're having trouble making the cups spin, make sure the thumbtack isn't pushed too far into the eraser.)

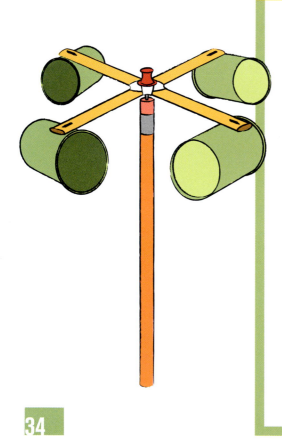

MEASURE *the wind*

Use a marker or pen to draw bold markings on one of the four cups. The marking could be a letter, a circle, or any other large shape. The mark will help you measure the wind once the cups start spinning.

Take your anemometer outside. Hold it up to the wind with one hand. The cups should spin. With your other hand, hold your watch or timer, and set it for one minute. (If it's not a windy day, you can supply the wind by blowing on the cups!)

As soon as the seconds start counting, *you* should start counting how many times your anemometer's cups spin around. Do this by watching the one marked-up cup. Watch that cup as the anemometer spins, and keep track of how many times *that* cup goes around in a complete circle. Keep counting until the minute is up!

And there you have it! You've measured the wind speed in *revolutions per minute*, or rpm. (A revolution is one complete circle.) Meteorologists use similar instruments to measure the wind's speed. Knowing how fast the wind is blowing helps meteorologists predict the weather.

One, Two, Three...

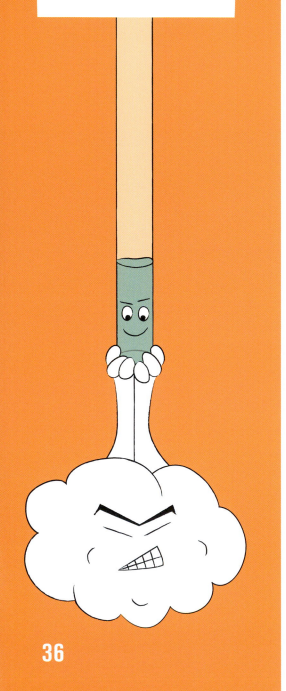

HOW DOES AIR PUSH?

DID YOU KNOW that you live in an "ocean" of air? It's true! You can't see, smell, or taste air. But, like water, air is a fluid. It has weight. The weight of air from the top of the sky presses down on the layers of air near the ground. This weight causes *air pressure*. This means that when you try to push your way through air, the air pushes back.

Air is much lighter than water—that's why you fall through air much faster than you sink in water. But you can feel the air pushing against you when the wind blows. When skydivers open their parachutes, air pressure pushes against the wide fabric of the parachutes, slowing their fall.

Now, you might not think that air can push very hard. But there's a lot of air near the surface of the Earth. In this activity, you'll see for yourself how hard this air can push. It turns out, air can push even harder than gravity can pull!

MATERIALS

- Clear drinking glass or cup
- Plastic drinking straw
- Water
- Piece of stiff, flat cardboard
- Sink or large pan

CAPTURE WATER *in a straw*

Fill the glass with water. Put the straw in the glass. Put your finger over the top of the straw. Then slowly lift the straw out of the glass. Make sure you do this over a sink or outside where it's safe to spill water.

You would think the water in the straw would fall out of the bottom. But it stays put—as long as you keep your finger on top of the straw. You've captured the water in your straw.

RELEASE *the water*

Make sure you hold the straw over a sink, bucket, or outside, and lift your finger from the top of the straw. The water should fall out.

Why does the column of water in the straw stay put when you hold your finger over the top? The answer is a little complicated. But a big reason is *air pressure*—the force of air pushing against objects. Remember that air is a fluid. When you move through air, the air pushes back—just like water in a swimming pool. So in order for the water in the straw to fall, it would have to push its way down through the air below it. And the air below the straw pushes *up* against the water inside the straw.

Now, when the *top* of the straw is open, all the air above the straw pushes *down* on the water. This downward push cancels out the upward push beneath the straw, so gravity can pull the water down. But when you block the top of the straw with your finger, you're shielding the water from the air pressure above it. No air can push down through the top of the straw with your finger in the way. So the only forces acting on the water now are gravity and the *upward* push of the air pressure beneath it. And as you can see, the air can push *up* harder than gravity can pull *down*!

Capture even **MORE WATER**

Now, try to hold water in a vessel much larger than the straw—the glass. Fill the glass with water again, nearly to the top. Completely cover the top of the glass with the piece of cardboard. (Note: If the cardboard is too soft or thin, the experiment won't work— the water will soak through.)

Air pressure can cause many changes to the weather. For example, winds are caused by the flow of air from an area of high air pressure to an area of low air pressure. Scientists who study weather can measure air pressure using a tool called a *barometer*. They use barometers to detect changes in air pressure. In most cases, a change in air pressure means the weather will change soon.

DEFY *gravity*

Working near a sink or outside, hold the cardboard tightly against the glass rim. Then, quickly, turn the glass and cardboard upside down. Some water may spill out—this is normal.

Now take your hand away from the cardboard. It may take you a few practice tries, but you should be able to hold the glass upside down, without the cardboard or the water inside falling out.

What's going on? It's the same situation as the water in the straw. No air can push down the water inside the upside-down glass—the bottom of the glass is in the way, just like your finger was in the way with the straw. So the air pressure *below* the glass pushes up with a greater force than gravity can drag the water down.

But why the cardboard? After all, you didn't need to cover the bottom of the straw with anything to get it to stay put. But if you tried turning the glass of water upside down *without* the cardboard, it would just spill.

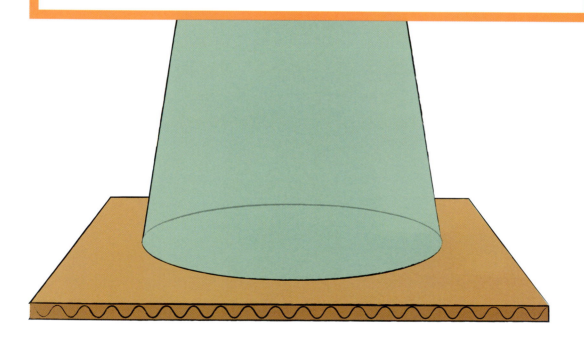

Besides air pressure,

another force is at work here, too: *surface tension*. As a liquid, water forms a *surface*. The surface of water acts sort of like the surface of a trampoline. When you push down against a trampoline, the trampoline stretches a bit, but it doesn't break apart. Water surfaces also stretch and bounce back against forces that push against them—but only up to a point.

Surface tension is why you don't need a piece of cardboard to hold water in a straw. The water at the bottom of the straw forms a surface. And because the straw is so narrow, this surface is strong enough to counteract gravity. A drinking glass, on the other hand, is much too wide for water to form a strong enough surface. That's why you need the piece of cardboard to hold the water in the upside-down glass. The cardboard helps keep the water's surface tension—while air pressure holds up both the cardboard and the water.

AXEL'S POWER SOURCE

Mollie looked back to her grandfather's manual.

Axel is a self-contained automaton. His rounded shapes allows for aerodynamic movement, while his slender arms and legs can twist and bend amazingly to fit into even the smallest of areas. Axel is an intelligent creature, complete with the functions of sight, speech, movement, and memory. The instructions below detail my every step in creating and using this copper machine. My greatest invention is invaluable to society and I estimate some day there will be thousands of types of Axels roaming about.

"Grandfather was a smart scientist, and his instructions are so complete. I hope I can help reboot Axel. What's first? Grandfather suggests first powering-up Axel. Let's see... Oh! Here's Axel's power button."

Mollie pushed the button, but Axel didn't move. She pushed it again, and still nothing happened.

Power
Axel should be alive and well, moving about, as a robot should. But, in the occasion that Axel appears immobile, check his source of power: the battery pack located in his chest cavity.

"I found your battery, Axel, just where it should be. This reminds me of a homemade battery I once made, but yours is more complex. I remember that electrons should flow in a circuit, but your circuit isn't closed. Let's re-clip this here and..."

Axel suddenly moved! His body stood tall, his head lifted, and his arms and legs wiggled to life! Feline rushed over to examine his new friend.

"Yes! Step one is complete! The power is restored."

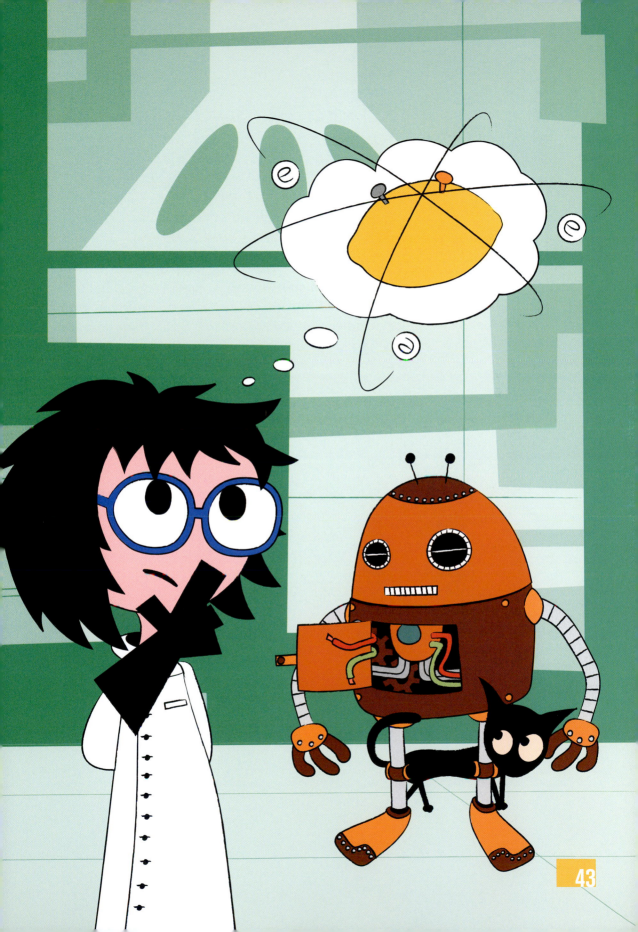

43

FRUIT-POWERED BATTERY

BATTERIES come in all shapes and sizes. They provide electric power for a great variety of gadgets. But how do batteries work? And how can you make a battery out of a lemon? To answer this question, you have to know a little bit about *electric currents*.

An electric current is a flow of tiny particles called *electrons*. These electrons flow easily through metal wires. The electrons also carry energy. The energy in electric currents is what powers things like light bulbs, phones, and computers. You can almost think of an electric current like a strong flow of water—but unlike rivers and waterfalls, electric currents *only* flow around in loops. These loops are called *circuits*.

You know how electronic gadgets have on and off switches? Those switches work by opening and closing gaps in the circuit loop. Switching "off" makes a gap in a circuit, so no current can flow. Switching "on" closes the circuit, and current will flow—but only if a power source, like a battery, pushes the current.

Chemical reactions at both ends of the battery, called the anode and the cathode, are the source of a battery's power. They act sort of like pumps that push the electric current around the circuit. The anode pushes the electrons out. The cathode pulls them back in. The exact chemical reactions vary from battery to battery. But you don't need anything too advanced to get an electric current flowing. In this activity, you'll use an ordinary lemon to make your own battery!

MATERIALS

- 1 lemon
- 1 copper nail or a clean penny
- 1 zinc or galvanized nail ("galvanized" means coated with zinc)
- 1 small LED light
- 2 electrical wires with clamps
- Electrical multimeter (optional)

Prepare THE FRUIT

Roll the fruit around roughly on a table or in your hands. Don't break the fruit's outer skin. Your goal is to squish the inside of the fruit a bit, to get its juice flowing.

The juice is important, because it's *acidic*. Acids react strongly with metals. Remember that a battery's power comes from chemical reactions at the anode and the cathode. Your anode and cathode are made of metal—zinc and copper. It's the reactions between the fruit's acid and these metals that move the electric current around the circuit.

Caution!

Use caution in this experiment. Electricity is dangerous. Make sure an adult is present. And do not eat any fruits or vegetables you use as batteries!

MAKE *the anode*

Push the zinc nail into the fruit. Congratulations! You've just made an *anode*. The acid in the fruit reacts with the zinc, dissolving it. Under the right circumstances, this reaction strips off electrons from the zinc atoms.

The anode is the part of the battery that pushes electrons out into the circuit. Normally, electrons don't like to be by themselves. They're usually stuck to the cores of *atoms*, the building blocks of matter. At the anode, a chemical reaction gets these electrons unstuck from their atoms. It sends them out from the battery and into the circuit's wire. (On batteries you buy at the store, the anode usually is marked with a minus [–] sign.)

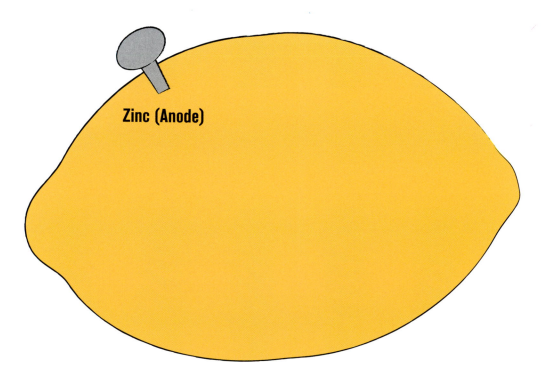

Zinc (Anode)

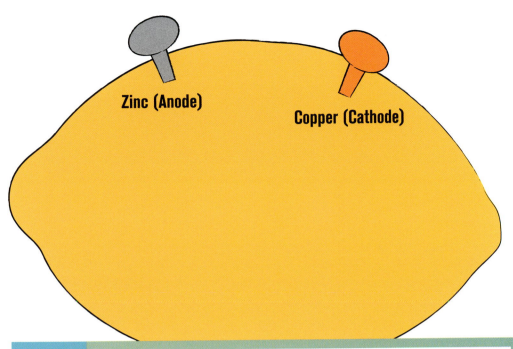

Zinc (Anode)

Copper (Cathode)

Make the CATHODE

Push the copper nail into the fruit about an inch away from the zinc nail. (If you're using a penny, cut a small slit into the fruit and push the surface of the penny in sideways. Make sure to leave about half the penny exposed.) You've just made a *cathode*. The cathode is the part of the battery that sucks electrons back in, after they've traveled around the circuit. A chemical reaction at the cathode helps draw the electrons back into the battery material. (On store-bought batteries, the cathode usually is marked with a plus [+] sign.)

Electrons flow very easily through copper—this is why many wires are made of copper. In the battery, the copper acts sort of like a straw. The acid reacts with the copper to draw the electrons back into the battery.

Complete THE CIRCUIT

You have an anode and a cathode. But your circuit isn't closed yet. Your electrons need a path to follow as they flow out from the zinc anode and back into the copper cathode. And this path has to connect to the LED light.

You'll use the two electrical clamp wires and the LED light to connect the circuit. (Hint: The pathway between the lemon, the wires, and the light should be a circle, and the wires should not cross.) Many LED lights have two small connecting spikes. Find the spike that sticks out from the flat side of the LED. Using one of the electrical wires, clamp one side to this spike, and clamp the other end of the wire to the zinc nail anode.

Using the second electrical wire, clamp one end to the other LED spike, and clamp the other end to the copper nail or penny cathode.

Your circuit is now complete and the light should be on! (If your light doesn't come on, you may have connected your wires to the wrong spikes on the LED. Try connecting the wires to the opposite spikes, and your circuit should work.)

Remember, electric currents only flow in a closed circuit. The parts of this circuit are: (1) the fruit battery, (2) the light, and (3) the wires connecting the light to the battery. These parts have to form a complete loop. Once the circuit is complete and closed, the light should glow.

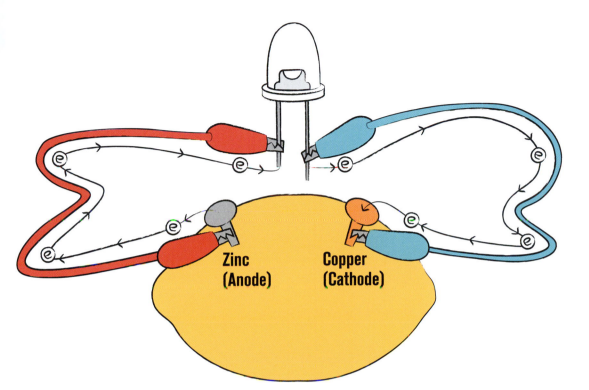

Zinc (Anode)

Copper (Cathode)

Electrolytes

In your fruit battery, the acidic juice acts as an *electrolyte*. An electrolyte in a battery is sort of like a bridge between the anode and cathode. Chemicals in the electrolyte help cause both reactions.

Acids are just one type of electrolyte. Other electrolytes are made of bases (the opposite of acids). Alkaline batteries use bases as their electrolytes. And still other batteries use salts. Lithium-ion batteries, which are used in many kinds of phones and portable computers, use salts as their electrolytes.

EXPERIMENT *further*

Try different types of fruits and vegetables as batteries. Lemons, oranges, and grapefruits all contain a type of acid called *citric acid*— that's why they taste sour. But there are other kinds of acids. Potatoes, for example, contain *phosphoric acid*. They can act as batteries, too.

If you have a multimeter for testing batteries, ask an adult to help you test how much power is being produced. Which fruits and vegetables produce the most power?

REAL-LIFE ROBOTS: Robo-Power

Many robots today work in factories. They don't need batteries because they run on the same electricity that powers the rest of the factory. For robots that are "unplugged," though, having a good battery is incredibly important. A good robot battery has to be both powerful and light. If the battery doesn't have enough power, then the robot won't be able to move. But if the battery is too heavy, then the robot will have to waste too much of its energy lugging around the extra weight.

Some robots, such as floor-cleaning robots, use nickel-metal hydride (NiMH) batteries. Others use lighter, more powerful lithium-ion batteries, which are also found in most portable computers and cell phones. Both of these batteries are rechargeable. Robots that are sent to explore other planets and moons—and outer space—are equipped with even more powerful batteries. These robots use radioactive elements, like *plutonium*, for power. Plutonium is an incredibly dense substance that gives off energy all the time. For example, the Cassini space probe, launched in 1997, uses plutonium for power. It traveled all the way to the planet Saturn to take the beautiful picture you see here.

Energy from plutonium can be dangerous on Earth. But in space, the robots use the energy to make electric power. These batteries can last for decades!

COMPARE FLOWERING PLANTS

WE SEE PLANTS like flowers, grass, and trees nearly every day. Plants grow in almost every part of the world—on mountaintops, in the oceans, and even in deserts! Plants have certain things in common: They have roots in the soil, parts that are green, and many have flowers and seeds. But all plants need water to live. In this experiment you will discover how the nutrients in water help plants to grow!

MATERIALS

- Newspaper
- 2 small flowerpots
- Masking tape
- Marker
- Gardening gloves (optional)
- Small pebbles or rocks
- Potting soil
- Shovel (optional)
- Marigold seeds
- Watering can or cup
- Water
- Liquid plant food
- Measuring spoons
- Ruler
- Pencil
- Paper

Caution!

Planting supplies, like soil and plant food, contain nutrients only plants should eat—and not you! Ask an adult to help you plant and water the seeds. Be sure that you do not touch your eyes or mouth after handling the planting materials!

LABEL *the pots*

Find a flat surface to use as your workspace and spread plenty of newspapers to cover the area. Newspapers will help protect your space from spilled water and dirt. If it's a nice day, you can work outdoors, but if you need to be inside, check with an adult to be sure you choose a good workspace.

Tear off two pieces of masking tape and put one piece on each flowerpot. (If you can't find flowerpots, you could also use large plastic cups.) Using the marker, label the tape on the first pot "No Plant Food." On the second pot's tape, write "Plant Food." These labels will help you later, after you've planted the seeds and begin the watering process.

Plant the **SEEDS**

If you're using gardening gloves, put them on now! (Wearing gloves isn't necessary, but it will help protect your hands from any spilled soil or plant food.)

Place small pebbles or rocks in the bottom of each flowerpot. Each pot should have the same number of pebbles, and they should form one layer on the bottom of the pot. Next, use a small shovel, spoon, or your hands to fill each pot about two-thirds full with potting soil. Make sure that each pot is filled to the same level.

Put four marigold seeds in each pot. (Note: If you can't find marigold seeds, sunflower seeds are a good replacement.) Be careful to select seeds that are full and round. Ones that look shriveled or discolored should not be used. Use your hands or the shovel to gently mix the seeds in with the top of the soil. Add just a little more soil to each pot to be sure that all of the seeds are completely covered by soil. Your seeds are now planted!

MIX *the water*

Now that both pots have flower seeds planted, you can see how the nutrients in water help the plants to grow. Fill the watering can or cup with water. Take the pot labeled "No Plant Food" and water it until the soil is just damp. You want the soil to be wet to the touch, but not too wet that extra water sits on the top of the soil.

After the first pot is watered, add a small amount of liquid plant food to the water in the can. (Hint: Use ¼ teaspoon of liquid plant food for every 4 cups of water in your can.) Using this water and plant food mixture, water the second pot labeled "Plant Food" with about the same amount of water as the first pot. Remember to not overwater the seeds! Dump out any extra water. Do not put any of this water mixture in the "No Plant Food" pot. Why?

Well, you know that plants need water to grow. But if one pot gets only plain water and the other has water plus liquid plant food, how does the extra food affect growth? That's why we planted two pots—to compare the results!

The "No Plant Food" pot, seeds, and plain water will act as a *control*—that is, the part of the activity that stays the same. You can compare the control to the *variable*. The "Plant Food" pot, seeds, and water mixture are the variable— the part of the experiment that you change on purpose to find a specific result. When you compare the control to the variable, it shows you how much the variable affects the activity. So, for plants, you can see how much the liquid plant food affects the plant's growth.

NO PLANT FOOD

PLANT FOOD

Let them GROW

After each pot is planted and watered, bring the pots indoors and set them side-by-side in a sunny spot near a window. You'll need the pots with their seeds to stay put for the next three to eight days. The seeds need to get settled into the soil and soak in the water before sprouting, so practice patience!

During this time, you'll want to check on your pots every day. Keep an eye on the moisture of the soil. Each day, touch your finger to the top of the soil to see how much moisture is there. If the soil feels dry, it's time to water the seeds again. Remember to water the "No Plant Food" pot with plain water, and the "Plant Food" pot with the special liquid plant food and water mixture. It is important not to mix up the watering method for each pot—it could change your results!

As you observe your pots, you can also keep a record to log growth. Divide your paper into two columns—with one writing area for each flowerpot. Record the date that you planted the seeds, and make a note every time you water each pot. Note which flowerpot is the control and which is the variable. You can also write other observations, such as the amount of sunlight shining through the window, or how the soil looks on a particular day.

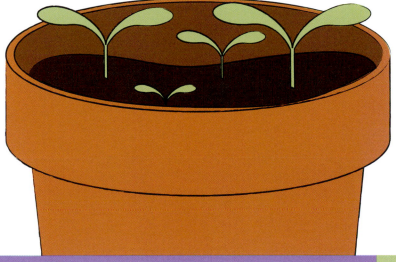

Watch them **SPROUT**

One day you'll notice that the first seed has sprouted! Watch for a tiny green stem or leaves to peak out from the top of the soil. Record the date that each seed sprouts. You'll also want to note how many seeds sprout from the four planted in each pot. Use a ruler to measure the height of each sprout. If a seed has not reached the surface by the 14th day, it most likely will not sprout.

Take note of which seeds sprouted first—was it the seeds given plain water, or the seeds given the water-and-food mixture? Why do you think that is?

Record the HEIGHT

Keep observing your plants every day, checking the moisture of the soil and continuing the same watering pattern. Using the ruler, measure each plant's height once per week for one month. Over time, you'll see your plants grow from a tiny seed to a familiar plant. These weekly measurements will show you which plants grew taller or faster than others. You might even notice the plant grow its leaves or form a flower bud!

COMPARE *the growth*

Look at your record log and evaluate how the "No Plant Food" seeds grew as compared to the "Plant Food" seeds. See if you can find any trends in the data you collected, like sprouting dates, or height of the plants.

Your seeds received the same treatment—the same type of pot, the same soil, and the same caretaker—but some seeds probably grew faster than others. Why? Is it because of the nutrients in the liquid plant food that you added to one of the pots? Here, the seeds in the pot that was given the plant food—the variable—most likely sprouted first because of the extra nutrients that they received. The control seeds, "No Plant Food," likely still sprouted and grew tall, but at a slower pace. By comparing the variable to the control, you can see that the liquid plant food added to the water helped the seeds to sprout and grow faster than plain water. Plants absorb the water—and any nutrients or substances in the water—to help them grow. *Pollutants* in the environment, such as dangerous chemicals, can get into the water supply and hurt the growth of a plant. It all depends on what's in the water source!

PLANT FOOD

NO PLANT FOOD

MAKE A WATER FILTER

YOU USE WATER every day—when taking a shower, cooking breakfast, or washing laundry. The water that pours from your faucets is likely clear in color and safe to use and drink. But how did it get that way? The water you use comes from bodies of water, from rainwater, or from water stored underground. It might look clean, but water from all types of sources should be *filtered* before people can use it. A filter uses a barrier to remove unwanted materials, such as dirt and germs, from the water.

In this activity, you'll form a homemade water filter to help you see how water from the environment is filtered for our use! Here's what you'll need:

MATERIALS

- Large, clear plastic soft-drink bottle (no lid needed)
- Wide-mouth jar
- Scissors
- Cotton balls
- Clean water
- Dirt
- Small, clean pebbles
- Clean sand
- Pitcher

PLACE *the bottle*

Select a flat surface as your workspace and spread newspapers to cover the area. Newspapers will help protect your space from any spilled water, pebbles, or sand. Set the empty jar in the center of the newspapers.

Ask an adult to help you cut off the bottom of the bottle, about 7 inches (18 centimeters) away from the top of the bottle. Recycle the bottom part of the bottle—you won't need it again! Turn the top part of the bottle upside down and set it in the jar. Make sure that the top of the bottle does not touch the bottom of the jar, but hangs somewhere in the center. The bottle should rest freely on the mouth of the jar.

Caution!

Although your homemade water filter takes much of the dirt from the water, the water is still not safe to use! Never drink the water that you filter in this activity. It may look clean but it might still have dirt or germs in it!

LAYER *the filter*

Once your bottle is in place, it's time to layer the filter materials! First, push a wad of cotton balls into the entire neck of the bottle. Add more cotton to form the first layer, about 1-inch (2.5 centimeters). Next, add a few handfuls of small, clean pebbles to form a 1-to-2 inch (2.5 to 5 centimeter) thick layer on top of the cotton. Last, pour clean, dry sand right on top of the pebbles to form a 2-inch (5-centimeter) layer. After these three layers, your bottle should be about halfway to three-fourths full.

Placing many layers of *porous* (absorbent) materials in the filter will help to remove the debris in the water as it slowly moves downward. These materials are able to absorb or keep back the unwanted materials, preventing them from passing through the layers. This helps to clean the water. In real water filtration plants, similar materials, such as crushed rocks, are used to filter water.

POUR *dirty water*

Fill a pitcher with clean tap water. Scoop some dirt into the water. Watch as the dirt spreads throughout the water, changing the color of the water from clear to brown. This dirty water is similar to the water found in nature—they both have debris that needs to be cleaned out before people can use it.

Carefully pour the dirty water into your water filter, allowing it to pass through the sand layer first. Slowly, keep pouring water on top of the sand layer in your filter and watch what happens!

WATCH *it filter*

Watch the water trickle down through the filter's layers. What happens to the layers as the water moves through them? Does the water move quickly or slowly? Does any air escape in the form of bubbles? What does the water look like when it leaves the filter?

As you probably will see, the dirty water steadily moves through the layers and eventually drips down through the cotton, out of the filter, and drops into the jar. The water that comes out looks much cleaner than it did when you poured it in. Where did the dirt go?

When the dirty water moves downward through the bottle filter, the unwanted materials in the water are too large to pass through and are caught within the layers. The rest of the water continues to filter through to the next layer and the next layer, with more dirt catching in each layer. The water keeps moving downward until it finally reaches the very bottom of the filter and drips into the jar. It just went through a *filtration* system! Large water filtration plants put dirty water through many more steps before it is ready to be used. The plants might filter water several times in a row, or even add safe chemicals that help to kill unwanted germs!

The water you filtered is not clean enough to drink, but it is much clearer than it was before. Even though you can't drink this water, you can still use it to water your flowers or houseplants! To experiment more, try pouring your filtered water through the bottle filter a second time. Does this make the water look even cleaner?

CREATE YOUR OWN FOSSILS

IF YOU'VE SEEN a *fossil*—or at least a picture of one—you know that fossils are extremely old! A fossil is the mark or remains of an organism that lived thousands or millions of years ago. Some of the best-known fossils include leaves, shells, or skeletons that were preserved after a plant or animal died.

Paleontologists have found most fossils in *sedimentary rocks*. Paleontologists are scientists who study life of prehistoric times by looking at fossils of plants and animals. The fossils formed from plant or animal remains that were quickly buried in *sediments*—the mud or sand that collects at the bottom of rivers, lakes, swamps, and oceans. Over time, these sediments became buried under other sediments. The upper sediments pressed down on the layers of mud and squeezed them into compact rock layers. Paleontologists have pieced together much of the story of Earth's past by examining its huge fossil record!

In this activity, you will recreate this fossilization process, by making your own mold fossil and examining the fossil and its imprint!

MATERIALS

- Newspaper
- Shell
- Paper towels
- Petroleum jelly
- Homemade plaster (recipe below)
- Large paper cup
- Sand

HOMEMADE PLASTER

- 3 cups flour
- 1 cup warm water
- Large mixing bowl
- Wooden spoon

STEP 1

Smear the SHELL

Select a flat surface as your workspace and spread newspapers to cover the area. Newspapers will help protect your space from any spilled jelly or plaster. Place a few paper towels down on the newspapers. Then, set your shell on top. The shell will serve as the animal that lived millions of years ago! (If you can't find a shell, you can also use a bumpy rock, old key, or a small toy.) Smear the petroleum jelly all over your shell. Make sure the entire surface is covered on all sides with the petroleum jelly. Set the paper toweling and shell to the side.

Mix homemade **PLASTER**

Next you'll mix homemade plaster—the material that will act like sedimentary rocks! You can make a kind of plaster at home with flour and water. This recipe makes a few cups of plaster. If you need more, simply double the recipe. You can also purchase plaster mix from most craft stores and follow the directions on the package.

Over the newspapers, first, combine 3 cups of flour and 1 cup of warm water in a large bowl. Stir the mixture with a wooden spoon for 1 minute. (Make sure it's smooth—no lumps!) Knead the mixture with your hands for about 5 minutes. If the plaster seems too thick, add more water 1 tablespoon at a time. If it seems too soupy, add more flour. Never pour the plaster down the sink because it can clog the pipes. Discard any leftover plaster in the trash or in a compost bin.

Once you've made a batch of plaster, quickly pour the mixture into the paper cup, about half way to the top.

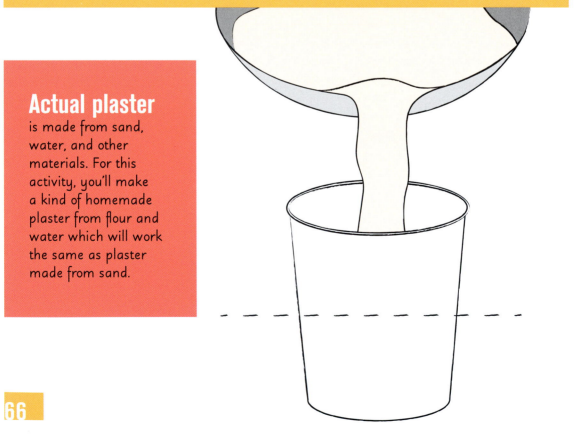

Actual plaster is made from sand, water, and other materials. For this activity, you'll make a kind of homemade plaster from flour and water which will work the same as plaster made from sand.

COVER *the shell*

Take the shell and put it directly into the plaster in the cup. Wiggle it down through the plaster a bit, but be sure that you can still see the top of the shell. Do not bury it in the plaster! Then, sprinkle a thin layer of sand over the shell and plaster, about 3/4 inch (about 2 centimeters) deep. Make sure you completely cover the shell and the plaster in the cup. The sand layer acts as another layer of sediment that covers your fossil.

Now, use the rest of the plaster you made and pour it on top of the sand layer. Cover the sand completely. The second layer of plaster should reach nearly to the top of the cup. Let your plaster-filled cup sit to dry for at least two hours.

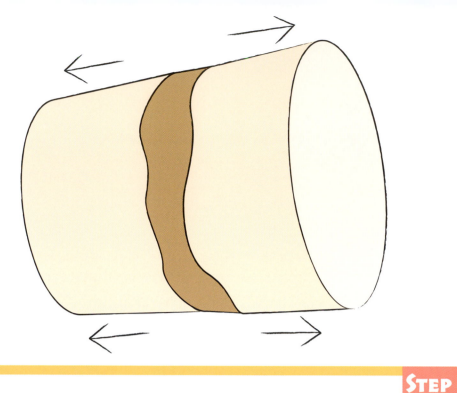

DISCOVER *the fossils*

When paleontologists think they may have discovered a fossil in rock, they work together to uncover the fossil—and see if there are any more nearby! Different fossils require different collecting techniques. Fossils of shells, teeth, and bones preserved in soft sand or mud are easiest to collect. Paleontologists can dig out these fossils with a shovel or remove them by hand.

Now it's your turn to uncover your fossils! When the plaster is dry to the touch, work over your newspaper covered area to tear the sides of the cup off of the plaster. Work slowly and carefully to remove all of the little bits of the cup from the plaster. Then, ask an adult to help you separate the layers of your rock. The top layer of plaster is separated from the bottom layer by the sand. Wiggle the two pieces to pull them apart.

Do you see your shell? Just like paleontologists, you'll have to find the best way to remove the shell from the rock. Ask an adult if they can pull it from the rock. You might have to use a pointy object, like a paper clip, to help lift the shell out of the plaster. Be careful that you don't harm the imprint in the plaster—this is part of the fossil you're looking for!

EXAMINE *the fossils*

Once the shell is removed, you can see that it made a mark in the plaster. Remember that fossils can be both a mark in the rock and the remains of an organism. Normally, paleontologists find either a mark or the remains, but yours is a unique case—you can examine both the shell and its mark.

Fossils help scientists discover what forms of life were present at different periods in Earth's past. Scientists spend a lot of time studying the fossils they find. They group fossils according to type and by location. *Dating*, or figuring out the age, of fossils is an important step in this process. Paleontologists want to know how old fossils are. Sometimes they can determine an exact date. Other times they have to guess.

You can examine your fossils in a similar way. Look at the lines and grooves created in the plaster fossil. Are there any areas where the grooves are deeper than others? Why do you think this might happen in real sedimentary rock layers?

Next, examine the shell fossil. Did the plaster change the shape of the shell? Did the plaster rock leave any residue behind? How do you think a paleontologist would clean the shell?

GROWING MOLD

MOLD! It's everywhere you don't want it to be—in your shower, on your feet, and on that leftover spaghetti in the fridge that you were planning on eating but maybe forgot about for a few days or weeks. But what is mold, and where does it come from?

Mold is a kind of *fungus*. Fungi (the plural of fungus) also include mushrooms and yeast. These organisms are *decomposers*. They get their food by breaking down plant and animal matter.

Like other fungi, molds develop from tiny particles called spores. Spores are so small that you often can't see them without a microscope. Mold spores may be tiny, but in this activity you will see that they can be found all over the place.

MATERIALS

- 2 small, clear jars with lids
- Banana peel
- Orange
- Slice of bread
- Plate
- Duct tape
- Spray bottle

Prepare your SPECIMENS

With the help of an adult, cut an orange into quarters. Take the orange outside and rub the pieces on a sidewalk or other firm structure where mold spores are likely to be. Do the same thing to the banana peel and slice of bread. Put the orange, banana peel, and bread on a plate, and leave it on the kitchen counter overnight.

Mold spores, too small to see with your naked eye, are found pretty much everywhere, especially outdoors. But these spores don't turn into mold unless they happen to settle on something that they can grow on. Remember, molds—like other fungi—are decomposers. Many spores may land on sidewalks, but sidewalks aren't the best places for molds to grow, because there's nothing on the sidewalk for them to decompose. Old pieces of food, on the other hand, make great homes for decomposers.

SEAL *your specimens*

The next day, place the banana peel and orange pieces in one of the clear jars. Spray the inside of the jar with water. Place the slice of bread in another jar. Lightly spray the inside of the jar with water. Why spray the food with water? Mold, like all living things, needs water to grow.

Screw the lids onto both jars. Seal the jars with duct tape. This tight seal prevents contaminants, like dust, from getting into the jars—and prevents the mold, once it grows, from getting out.

After you've sealed your specimens, wash the plate, countertop, and your hands with soap and warm water.

Mold with a heart of gold

Most mold looks gross, smells gross, and can make you sick if you eat it. But, you may be surprised how helpful mold can be.

As decomposers, molds play a vital role in ecosystems (areas of land and the organisms that live there). By breaking down dead organisms, molds help to fertilize the soil—which, in turn, helps plants grow. And without plants, we humans wouldn't have a food supply.

Penicillin is a prescription drug that comes from a mold. It was the first antibiotic—bacteria-fighting drug—used to treat serious diseases.

The strong flavor of blue cheese comes from a mold, which is visible as blue-green streaks in the cheese. Have you tried it?

STASH *your jars*

Place the jars in a warm, dark place. (Be sure that those around you know where you place the jars! You wouldn't want anyone throwing away your experiment by mistake!)

After one week, check your jars and see what is growing. You should see green or white fuzzy material. Leave the jars for another week and see what happens. How have the bread and fruit changed? What is happening inside the jar? Which pieces of food attract the most mold?

Remember, do NOT open the jars!

Wash and Recycle

The molds that grow could be dangerous, so do not open the jars at any time! Once the experiment is finished, the entire jar and contents could be thrown away. A more eco-friendly option is to have an adult help you clean and recycle the jars. Ask an adult to wear rubber dishwashing gloves and take off the tops of the jars. Empty all of the contents into a garbage bag and tie the bag tightly. Throw the sealed bag in the garbage. Take the jars and lids and wash them with hot, soapy water. Scrub thoroughly. The containers could also be put with detergent through a hot water wash cycle in the dishwasher. You may want to wash the containers twice, for good measure. After their soapy bath, the jars and lids can be dried and put in the recycling bin, or used again— maybe in another experiment!

AXEL'S SIGHT AND SPEECH

"Next is your sight and speech," Dr. Mollie Cule said, turning the page in the manual.

Sight
Eyeballs are intricate objects. Activated by the brightest of color in the rainbow, Axel's eyes only light up when exposed to such pigments.

Speech
While human language is difficult to grasp, I've programmed Axel using an advanced number system. Such programming allows for Axel to decode human speech, understand the meaning, and speak back to us. The more we interact with him, the speedier he understands and learns about the world. This innovative program is only productive when the number system is intact. Ensure all pieces are in place in his head. What an amazing method to communicate!

"These are pretty hard instructions, Grandfather," Mollie said as she pet Feline.

"Axel's sight can be activated by bright colors, like in the rainbow. And his speech uses a special coded system... I know I've seen these types of experiments before."

Mollie retrieved grandfather's Experiment Log from the table, flipping to *Learn Binary Language*.

"Perfect! I'll start here."

LEARN BINARY LANGUAGE

THE BINARY SYSTEM is a way of writing numbers with only two digits— 1 and 0. The word "binary" means "two at a time." In binary, 1's and 0's are called bits, which is short for binary digit. The binary system is very important in computer science. Computers and robots, like Axel, use binary numbers every day to "talk" to humans like you and me!

Normally, we write numbers with the decimal system. This system has ten digits—1, 2, 3, 4, 5, 6, 7, 8, 9, and 0. We humans probably developed the decimal system because we have 10 fingers to count with. Computers and electronic devices, on the other hand, don't have fingers. They count with tiny electronic switches called transistors. A transistor can switch either "on" or "off," like a light switch. These two states—on and off—can stand for 1 and 0.

A modern computer chip might have billions of transistors. That's a lot of bits! And those bits can stand for more than just numbers. Those 1's and 0's can *encode* (hold information) just about anything—words, pictures, videos, and software programs. Modern robots, too, run on electronic transistors, and those bits control how robots behave. You could say that binary is the native language of robots like Axel.

In this activity, you're going to make a string of six bits. By the end, you'll be able to use these bits to count and "speak" just like robots and computers!

MATERIALS

- Cardboard tubes (from 2 paper towel or 3 toilet tissue rolls)
- Scissors
- Hole punch
- Long piece of string
- 7 pieces of hollow dried pasta, such as rigatoni or penne
- Bold marker

Cut out YOUR BITS

Using scissors, cut the cardboard tubes into six short, equal-sized pieces. Be careful not to flatten them too much. These tubes will act like bits—binary digits, 1's and 0's. (Note: If you don't have paper towels or toilet tissue rolls to spare, you can also use the cardboard tube from aluminum foil, wax paper, or wrapping paper.)

STRING *your bits together*

Punch two holes through the middle of each tube with the hole puncher. Thread the string through a piece of dried pasta, and tie the string over and around the end piece of pasta to secure it. Then thread the string through both holes in one tube, then through another piece of dried pasta. (The pasta's purpose is to space out the cardboard tubes. If you don't have pasta, you could also use thick beads or cut straws.) Continue to thread the string, alternating the tubes and pasta. As you work, make sure there isn't much slack between the tubes and pasta. Once you've threaded all six tubes, thread an extra piece of pasta on the loose end. You should now have a piece of pasta on each end of your six-tube setup.

Tie the string over and around the last end-piece of pasta to secure everything together. There should be knots on both ends of your bit string. Cut off any extra string.

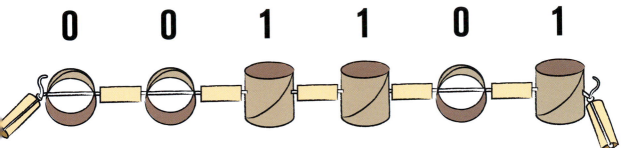

0 0 1 1 0 1

FLIP *"on" and "off"*

Remember that computers use binary numbers because they count with tiny switches called transistors. When a transistor switch is "on," it stands for "1." When it's "off," it stands for "0."

Your cardboard tube bits are switches, too. When a cardboard tube is upright, it's "on." It stands for "1." When it's lying on its side, it's "off," and stands for "0." The bits should even look like ones and zeros, based on how they're lying or standing.

Flip your switches to read 0 0 1 1 0 1 in binary. (Look at the illustration for help.) Got it? Great job! Now try 1 0 1 0 0 1 on your own.

Mark PLACE VALUES

Now that you know how to flip your switches "on" and "off" to stand for 1's and 0's, you can use these binary number bits to count to ten. Just like real computers, you can encode the 1's and 0's to add up to many different numbers. But first, you have to understand exactly how those 1's and 0's represent numbers.

Stand all of the cardboard tubes upright. Using a marker, write the following numbers on the front of the tubes in this order, from left to right:

32 — 16 — 8 — 4 — 2 — 1

These numbers are place values. You might be familiar with place values already, since the decimal system uses them too. Each digit has a value based on its place in a row. In a decimal number, from right to left, those places are "ones, tens, hundreds, and thousands." These decimal number place values are all based on multiplying the number 10. For example, the "thousands (1,000)" place value is 10 x 10 x 10.

Let's look at the decimal number 2,805. This number means "2 thousands, 8 hundreds, no tens, and 5 ones." You find this number by adding all of these place values together.

Place values work the same way in a binary number—except binary number place values are based on multiplying the number 2, not 10. For example, the "4" place value is 2 x 2. The "32" place value is 2 x 2 x 2 x 2 x 2. These binary place values work the same way as the place values in the decimal system. You can find a number by adding all of these place values together.

This is why you wrote the numbers 32 — 16 — 8 — 4 — 2 — 1 on the tubes. These binary number place values will help you add using the binary number system!

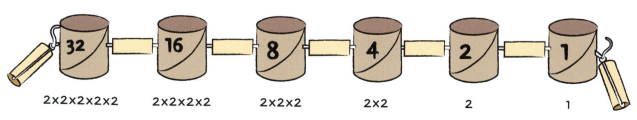

| 32 | 16 | 8 | 4 | 2 | 1 |
| 2x2x2x2x2 | 2x2x2x2 | 2x2x2 | 2x2 | 2 | 1 |

Count to ten IN BINARY

So how do you count to ten with only six switches? That's where place value comes in. Just like a decimal number, you find the total value of a binary number by adding together the place values.

So, for example, flip your tubes to read 0 0 1 1 0 1 in binary. Using what you know about the binary system and place values, find the total value in decimal numbers. (Hint: Add together the place value numbers written on the outside of the tubes to find out!)

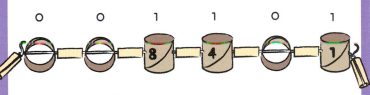

$$0 + 0 + 8 + 4 + 0 + 1 = 13$$

Look at the numbers in the column to the right. These numbers show how to count to ten using binary numbers. So, 7 is 111 in binary.

That looks a little strange, doesn't it? Binary takes some getting used to—for humans, at least. Now you try! You can make each of these binary numbers on your bit string and add up the place values. Remember to first flip the tubes "on" for 1 and "off" for 0. Then, add up the place value numbers written on the tubes to find the answer. You'll see that each of these binary numbers adds up to 1, 2, 3, and so on, all the way to 10. (To count to 10 in binary, you won't need to use the two leftmost tubes here.)

1
10
11
100
101
110
111
1000
1001
1010

CODE *with binary numbers*

Computers don't just display 1's and 0's. They show us words, pictures, and videos. They even talk to us and play games with us. They can do all of these things because those 1's and 0's can act like a code.

Take the letters of the alphabet, for example. There are 26 letters in the English alphabet, from A to Z. So it's easy to just write each letter as a number. A is 1. Z is 26. E is 5, and so on. So, now that you know how to use place values to add up binary numbers, can you figure out how to write the English alphabet in binary numbers?

First, make a list of the letters in the English alphabet and their corresponding decimal number. Then, find each binary number that corresponds to each letter. For example, the letter "L" is number 12. The number 12, in binary, is 1100. So, "L" is 1100 in binary! Keep going until you can write all of the letters of the alphabet in binary code!

Congratulations! Now you can speak robot language! Can you write "AXEL" in binary? How about "MOLLIE"? (Answers below.)

Letter **Decimal** **Binary**

F = 6 = 110

Answers

English: A - X - E - L
Decimal: 1 - 24 - 5 - 12
Binary: 1 - 11000 - 101 - 1100

English: M - O - L - L - I - E
Decimal: 13 - 15 - 12 - 12 - 9 - 5
Binary: 1101 - 1111 - 1100 - 1100 - 1001 - 101

REAL-LIFE ROBOTS: Smart Robots

The way robots "think" is called *artificial intelligence*, or AI for short. The ultimate goal of AI research is to make a robot that can think like a human— all with a pattern of 1's and 0's! Scientists are still learning exactly how human brains process information or store memories. But brains appear to "compute" by using patterns of *neurons*—the individual cells that make up a brain. Your brain has trillions of neurons. In a way, these neurons act a bit like a robot's transistors, switching on or off to make certain patterns. When you answer a question in school, or talk with a friend, your brain's neurons are actually doing a whole lot of computing, really fast.

   All modern robots aren't as smart as humans. But some robots are pretty sharp. In 2011, for example, a computer named Watson beat two human champions in the trivia game show "Jeopardy!" Watson was not connected to the Internet. It had to "understand" the game show questions, consult its memory banks for clues, and answer faster than its human opponents. Not bad for a binary-speaking robot!

MAKE A RAINBOW

RAINBOW CONTROL

YOU'VE PROBABLY seen a rainbow before—it's an arc of colors that appears in the sky after it rains. But how does it mysteriously form? Rainbows appear when millions of raindrops are lit up by sunlight. A rainbow is not an object you can touch or feel, but actually a pattern of light. Light is made of waves of energy. These waves—just like ocean waves—can have different lengths. The different wavelengths appear to us as different colors.

Sunlight has a mixture of wavelengths that we see together as white light. The colors in sunlight, from the longest wavelength to the shortest, are red, orange, yellow, green, blue, indigo, and violet.

So, when sunlight—with its mixture of wavelengths—passes through a raindrop, the light is *refracted* (bent). Each wavelength bends at a certain angle. Light with the longest wavelengths bends the least and looks red. Light with the shortest wavelengths bends the most and looks violet. This is how the same pattern of colors forms in every rainbow in the sky!

But, did you know that you don't have to wait until it rains to see a rainbow? Light is refracted in the same way to create colorful arcs in other sprays of water, like in sea spray, garden hoses, or lawn sprinklers. You can actually make your own rainbow, too!

MATERIALS

- Flashlight
- Tall, clear drinking glass
- Water
- Large piece of white paper

FILL *the glass*

Find a tall drinking glass. It must be made of glass and be clear! Any designs etched into the glass may affect the outcome, so be sure that the glass is smooth! (If you can't find a smooth glass, you could also use a clear fishbowl, cereal bowl, or vase.) Fill the glass with room temperature water, about three-fourths of the way to the top. Set the glass on a table or countertop, not far from the edge.

FOLD *the paper*

Hold the piece of paper tall-ways, and fold it in half horizontally. The paper should look like a tent. Set the folded paper on the table. Place it about 4 inches (10 centimeters) behind the glass.

SHINE *the light*

Turn your flashlight on. Now, turn the lights off in the room. (Hint: If it's daytime, close the blinds or pull the curtains over the windows to darken the room even more.) Shine the light through the glass filled with water onto the white paper. Keep the flashlight about 6 to 8 inches (15 to 20 centimeters) away from the glass.

See the **RAINBOW**

Slowly tilt the flashlight up and down, moving it slightly from side to side. (Hint: Try holding the flashlight near the bottom of the glass, shining the light slightly upwards.) As you move the light, keep your eyes on the white paper and watch for the rainbow to appear! It's alright if you have to try tilting the flashlight a few times to find the rainbow—real rainbows need just the right conditions to appear!

Great job! You created your very own rainbow, just like in the sky. Here, the flashlight acts as sunlight, shining through the water in the glass— which acts like the raindrops. The glass bends the light through the water, which creates a colorful rainbow on your paper sky!

RAINBOW CONTROL

Gold at the End of the Rainbow?

Legend claims that if you find the end of a rainbow, there are riches, like gold coins and jewels, waiting. Others believe that reaching the end of a rainbow brings everlasting good luck. While those may be tempting offers, it is truly impossible to find the end of the rainbow! Why?

Remember that a rainbow is not a material object. It's just a pattern of light. And what's more, you are always at the center of the rainbow you see. If you move, the rainbow moves with you. And if you turn, so the sun is no longer behind you, the rainbow will vanish entirely. Trying to find the end of a rainbow, therefore, is a bit like chasing your own shadow!

STACKING LIQUIDS

STACKS of blocks, stacks of paper—these sorts of stacks make sense. But stacks of *liquids?* That probably sounds impossible.

But it's not impossible—it's science. You can stack liquids like you can stack bricks, just so long as you use the right liquids and put them in the right order.

Why? Different liquids have different *densities*. For example, a cup of honey weighs more than a cup of water—meaning that honey is denser than water. With some exceptions, denser stuff sinks through less dense stuff. So if you put layers of liquids in a tall glass, they'll arrange themselves in layers, with the densest stuff on the bottom and the least dense stuff on top.

MATERIALS

- Graduated cylinder or tall, narrow glass
- Honey
- Light corn syrup
- Dish soap (brightly colored works best)
- Water
- Vegetable oil
- Rubbing alcohol
- Food coloring

Layer your **SWEETS**

Honey is the densest liquid in this experiment, so it will be the bottom layer. Pour honey into your glass until it forms a layer that's about 1/6 of the glass's height.

Light corn syrup is less dense than honey, but denser than the rest of the liquids, so it goes in next. Pour the same amount of corn syrup over the honey. Because the corn syrup and honey are both so thick, they shouldn't mix much when you pour. Now you should have two visible layers—yellow honey on the bottom, clear corn syrup above.

Soap and **WATER**

Dish soap is going to be the next layer of your liquid stack. Squeeze out a layer on top of the corn syrup. Using a brightly colored dish soap will help you distinguish this layer from others.

Now for the water layer. First, pour some water in a liquid measuring cup and mix in some food coloring (make sure you use a different color than the dish soap). When your water is brightly colored, carefully pour it on top of the layer of dish soap. Unlike thick honey and corn syrup, water flows pretty easily and will mix with the dish soap if you're not careful. In any case, you're likely to end up with some bubbles. If you have a turkey baster, use that to suck up the water from your measuring cup and gently drop it on top of the soap layer. After everything settles, you should have four distinct layers—honey, corn syrup, dish soap, and water.

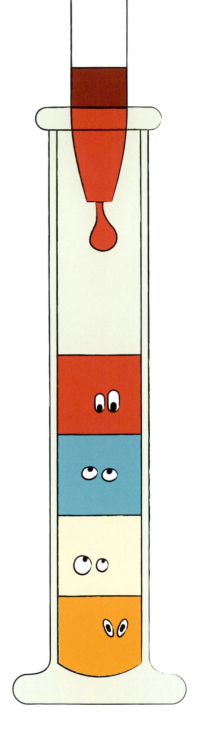

OIL *and alcohol*

Now for the really interesting part. Pour a layer of vegetable oil on top of the colored water. Again, be gentle—you don't want your oil to fall through the water layer and mix with the dish soap.

Rubbing alcohol is the least dense liquid that we'll be using, and it flows very fast. Because of this quality, you need to be especially careful when you pour it over the oil—it can easily stream right through and mix with the water underneath. Again, if you have a turkey baster, use it to pour more gently. And feel free to mix in another color of food coloring with the rubbing alcohol before you add it to the top.

And there you have it—six layers of liquids, neatly stacked according to their densities.

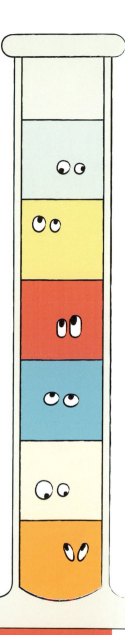

Miscibility

You may have heard the expression "oil and water don't mix." Well, it's true! Oil and water are not very *miscible*—that is, they don't mix easily. You can put oil and water together and stir and stir and stir, but the two liquids seem to repel each other. If you let them rest, the oil and water will separate back into layers.

Alcohol and water, on the other hand, are extremely miscible. In fact, if you poured alcohol straight into water, the two liquids wouldn't form layers at all. They'd just mix completely. That's why you need the layer of oil between the water and alcohol. The oil acts like a liquid wall between the miscible water and alcohol.

COLOR-CHANGING FLOWERS

YOU MAY KNOW that plants need water to live. But where do they get water from? After all, plants don't drink water like we do. You might think that plants "drink" water that falls as rain. But actually, raindrops mostly run down plants and drain into the soil.

The soil is where almost all plants get their water. Plants "drink" by pulling the water in the soil through their roots. From the roots, the water travels up the stem of the plant to its leaves and flowers. This water also contains minerals and other nourishing substances that plants need to live.

Imagine drinking water through your feet! Well, that's how plants do it, and in this activity, you'll prove that it's true.

MATERIALS

- 3 white carnations
- 3 clear plastic or glass cups
- Water
- 2 colors of food coloring
- Scissors

CAUTION: Make sure an adult is present to help you use scissors and other sharp tools carefully.

COLOR *the water*

Fill the cups at least halfway full of room temperature water. Be sure that the cup you choose will allow the flower to stand upright. Leave one cup with plain water. Put different food colorings in the two other cups. Don't skimp on the food coloring—you want the water to be brightly colored.

STEP 2

CUT *the flowers*

Using the scissors, cut the bottoms off of each flower stem at an angle. Cutting the stems at an angle means more of the stem's inside is exposed. The diagonal cut has a larger surface area than a straight-across cut. Working quickly, put each freshly cut flower into a cup, including the cup with the plain water. (This flower will serve as a point of comparison to those in the food-coloring water.)

Exposing the inside of the flower stem to the water is important because the stem works a bit like a sponge. If you put a dry sponge on top of a bowl of water, those holes draw the water up into the sponge. This process is called *capillary action*. A flower stem is also filled with many tiny tubes which work like the sponge's holes. Water is pulled up these tubes just like it's pulled into a sponge.

WATCH *the flowers*

Now comes the waiting game. Check back every few hours to see how your flowers are drinking. Within a day or so, the flowers should have "drank" water up through their stems—and if that water has food coloring, the flower petals should turn the same color. Some flowers might drink up colored water faster than others.

Plants don't just drink water from the soil. As you can see, they also drink substances dissolved in that water. Those substances can be healthy for the plant. Soil water contains minerals and nutrients that plants need to grow. But soil can also become polluted, or dirty. Can you guess what happens when plants grow on polluted land?

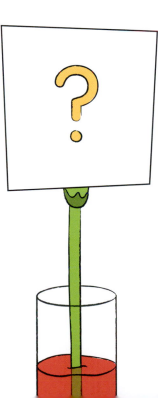

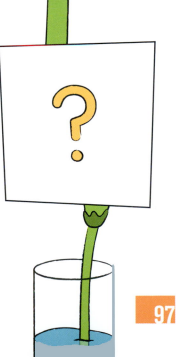

MAKE *multicolored flowers*

Remember the flower you put in plain water? The petals should still be plain white. Boring! Time to spice up that flower's life by adding not one but two colors to its petals!

Ask an adult to help you cut the white flower's stem vertically, so it's split in half down the middle like an unzipped zipper. Don't cut all the way up into the flower—you just want to split the stem about half way. Make the water and food coloring mixture in two new cups. Be sure each cup has a different color of water. Submerge each side of the stem into one of the colored water cups.

Wait and see how your white flower fares. Do the two colors blend evenly together on the flower? Or are the colors drawn to different sides of the petals? If so, why do you think that happens?

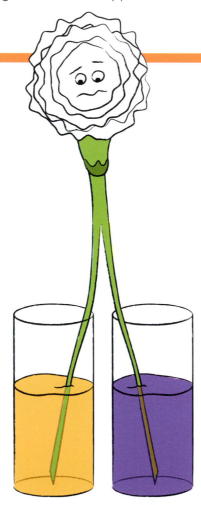

Dyeing Flowers

Florists often dye white flowers unusual colors, such as turquoise or plum, to create just the right look for an inventive floral design.

MOVING MOLECULES

EVERYTHING IS JIGGLING.

Don't let this fact alarm you. But everything—the ground, the air, this book you're reading, and even your own body—is made of very, very, very tiny bits of matter called atoms and molecules. (Hey, that sounds like Mollie Cule, doesn't it?) A molecule is a group of atoms. And these atoms and molecules just can't stop moving. They can't help it. All atoms and molecules have at least a little bit of energy, and this energy makes them randomly jiggle.

How much they jiggle, though, depends on how much energy they have. We measure this kind of energy as *temperature*. In other words, the hotter molecules are, the more they jiggle. Try this experiment to see how temperature affects the motion of molecules.

MATERIALS

- 2 large, heatproof glass containers
- Food coloring
- Boiling water
- Iced water

Make COLD WATER

A water molecule is made of two hydrogen atoms and one oxygen atom. That's why you sometimes see water written as "H_2O."

Fill one glass most of the way with cold water. Add a few ice cubes. Let the water stand for a few minutes. The ice will melt a bit and the liquid water will become extremely cold.

STEP 2

Make HOT WATER

Ask an adult to help you fill another glass with hot—almost boiling—water. You can heat up water in a pot or a tea kettle and pour it in the glass. Or you can just microwave the glass for one or two minutes. (If you're microwaving, be careful! Unlike in a pot, microwave-heated water can get really hot without looking like it's boiling.)

Cold   Hot

TEST *the jiggling*

Remove the ice cubes from the glass of cold water. Let the boiling water come to rest. If you have an unequal amount of water in the two glasses, carefully pour out the extra.

Working quickly, add a drop of food coloring to each glass, one right after the other. Watch the glasses carefully. (If you can, take a video!)

Notice that the food coloring isn't being mixed or stirred into the water. It should spread through the water on its own. This process is called *diffusion*. Diffusion happens because of the random jiggling of the water and food coloring. And, as you can see, diffusion happens much faster when a liquid's molecules are jiggling faster.

Solids, Liquids, and Gases

You probably know that most substances can be solid, liquid, or gas, depending on their temperature. But why? Well, it actually has to do with how much a substance's molecules jiggle.

Imagine molecules are kids in a school. During class, these molecule-kids act like solids. They sit in an orderly grid of desks. While sitting, the kids may move a little bit, to breathe, blink their eyes, scratch their hair, take notes. But they don't move enough to disrupt the grid shape of the classroom.

Now imagine a group of friends walking down the hallway. These molecule-kids are behaving like a liquid. They're moving much more than the kids stuck in a classroom! But the group of kids sticks together, mostly. The molecule-kids flow down the hallway all grouped together.

Gas molecules are the most jiggly of all. Have you ever gotten so hyper that you just want to run around a room, back and forth, wall to wall? That's what gas molecules do. They don't even stick together, like liquids do. They jiggle so much that they fly every which way, spreading out to fill a big space.

AXEL'S MOVEMENT

"So, Axel, can you see the colors? I know I tried some other interesting experiments along the way, but I hope I programmed your bits right," said Dr. Mollie Cule.

She looked down to read the manual, when another voice startled her: "Affirmative. All transistors are functional."

"AXEL! You can see me? You're talking!"

"Affirmative. All optical and voice recognition subroutines are functional. Axel is my self-designation code. Hello, human! What is your self-designation code?"

"Self-designation code … oh! I know what you mean. My name is Dr. Mollie Cule."

"Hello, Dock Tamale Cool!"

"Oh … maybe you should just call me Mollie."

"Hello, Mollie! What is your primary function?"

"My function? Well, I'm a scientist. I'm Doc U. Ment's granddaughter and I'm helping finish his master project. And I think I just did! Your power's on, you can see, and speak. I rebooted the robot! What else is there?"

"According to my power-on self-test, my systems are approximately 75 percent functional."

"Only 75 percent? But what's wrong?"

A loud whirring sound suddenly came from his chest.

"I cannot move," Axel answered.

"Yikes," Mollie said. "You're right. I haven't seen you move a muscle! Or ... whatever you have instead of muscles. Gears? I wonder how to fix that. Grandfather, what's next?" Mollie flipped to the next section called **Movement**.

Movement

My automaton is also able to walk, bend, and grasp items with its three "fingers."

Initiate the knee and other joints with a hardy slathering of Greasy Gears, my own secret liquid mixture made especially to mobilize robotic joints.

His arms and fingers are another challenge. While slender, his extremities are delicately interconnected. Originally, I planned to construct Axel with five fingers, reflecting his human counterparts, but only three fingers fit on his hand. My included sketches outline this five-fingered hand, but the mechanics work in the same manner. Axel now has three fingers, which I find even more fascinating for experimentation.

"I see the bottle of Greasy Gears on the shelf. Axel, I'll follow Grandfather's sketches to fix your fingers and then oil your joints. But, then I need to take a rest and have a snack...maybe I'll make us ice cream! Doing all of these scientific activities is filling up my brain—and emptying my stomach!"

"Affirmative, Mollie. Thank you."

"Okay, here goes!"

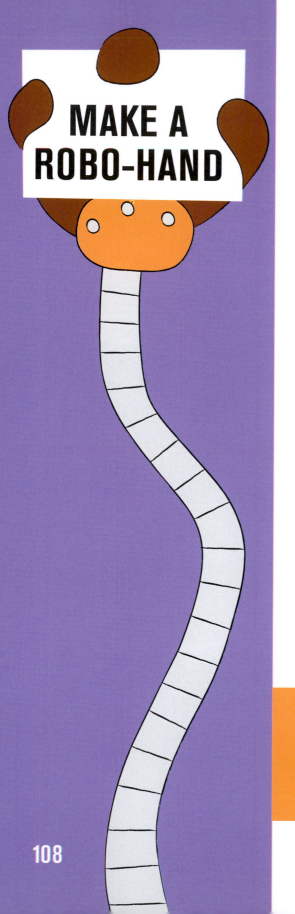

MAKE A ROBO-HAND

ROBOTS are often impressive inventions that perform amazing tasks. They help us with difficult missions like flying to space, building cars, or performing surgeries! But not all robots look the same. Some have wheels for feet, or a computer for a brain, or a camera lens for eyes! Many factory robots are made with big arms that have special tools on the ends instead of hands or fingers. Robots are made for very specific purposes, so they don't always need all the bells and whistles of a human hand—like four fingers and a thumb.

After all, look at all the things we humans can do with our hands! We can hold tools with our hands. We can grasp objects for pushing and pulling and throwing. We can write with pencils, hold books, and tap and swipe the touch screens on our phones.

But, some robots are being developed to mimic the movements of the human hand. The hand is so wonderful that you'd think it would be hard to make a robotic version of one. But actually, it's pretty simple! Here's what you'll need to make your own:

Caution!

Make sure an adult is present to help you use sharp tools carefully.

MATERIALS

- Blank sheet of paper
- Bold marker
- Pencil
- 10 plastic drinking straws
- Scissors
- Waxed dental floss, thick thread, or fishing line
- Thin cardboard, such as from a cereal box (for fingers)
- Thick cardboard, such as from a packing box (for rest of hand)
- Duct tape
- Cardboard tube, from a toilet tissue roll
- 5 small keychain rings (optional)
- Colored markers (optional)

Trace your **HAND**

Place your hand on a blank sheet of paper and trace its outline. If you have very small hands, you could to do this step with an adult's hand. Otherwise your robo-hand might be too small to work with.

Mark lines at all 14 joints—five knuckles, plus two joints per finger and one joint for the thumb. Now put five plastic straws on top of your hand-outline, placing one for each finger and the thumb. (Note: If your straws have a flexible end, place that end toward the wrist, not toward the fingertips.) The bottoms of the straws should be even at the wrist, so you'll need to cut the thumb and pinky straws down to size at the fingertip-ends.

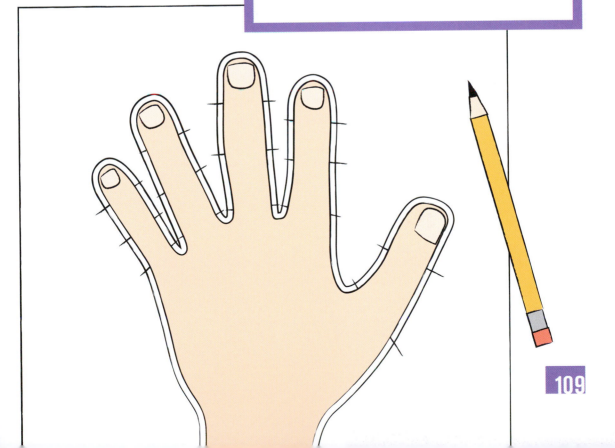

109

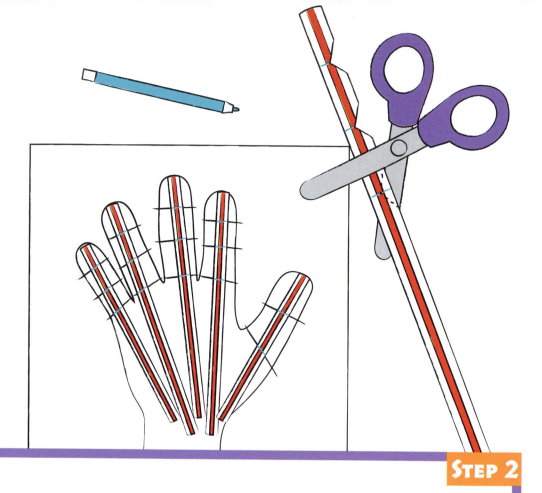

Cut out the JOINTS

Look at the way the straws line up with your hand-outline. Mark the straws at each spot where they overlap the finger and thumb joints— remember, there should be markings on the straws for five knuckles, plus two joints per finger and one joint for the thumb.

Use the scissors to cut diamond-shaped holes in the straws at each joint, as shown in the illustration. These holes will act as the inside of your finger joints and knuckles.

Cutting the holes can be a bit tricky. You want to cut deep enough that the straw bends easily, but not so deep that you risk cutting straight through the whole straw. Try to cut about 1/2 to 2/3 of the way through the width of the straw. Also, make sure that you cut all of the joints at the same angle, so they're all "facing" the same way. Note that the thumb will only have two holes, not three. When you're finished cutting, you will wind up with 14 total joint-holes.

Make the TENDONS

Divide the dental floss (or thread or fishing line) into five long strings, about four times as long as the straws. Thread one piece of floss through each straw, and tie each at its fingertip. To do this, pull the floss up through the top of the straw. Loop it around and under the first finger joint. Pull the looped floss up through the top of the finger again and tie a tight knot. This knot will secure the floss in place. The knot should sit about where your fingertip would be.

Once you have your knot, use scissors to cut thin strips of duct tape. Use the tape to secure the knots to the top sections of the straw (again, make sure the knots and the tape are about even with the fingertips).

After the string is tied and taped, test one finger by pulling on the other end of the string. The straw should bend inward at the joints, one by one. Repeat this process for each of the four fingers and the thumb.

Your human fingers work in the same way as the straws you've just constructed. Within each of your fingers is a strong string, called a *tendon*. The tendon connects to muscles in your forearm. When one of these muscles flex, it pulls the tendon—and the tendon, in turn, bends your finger inward.

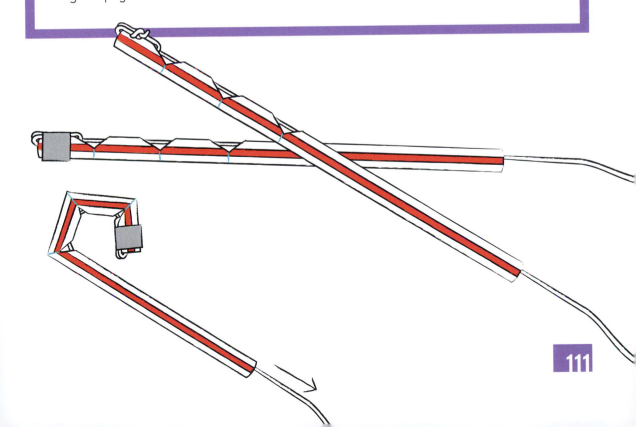

Make the **EXOSKELETON**

In a human hand, the tendons lay flat against your fingerbones. Of course, human bones are all wrapped up in skin. Robots don't need skin. So for simplicity's sake, you're going to make a robot hand with the skeleton on the outside—called an *exoskeleton*.

Cut five strips of thin cardboard about the width of your fingers. Cut each strip into three pieces, with each piece about the size of a finger joint. (Note: You'll only need two pieces for the thumb.) These cardboard pieces will form the bones on your hand's exoskeleton.

Using thin strips of duct tape, tape each piece of cardboard to the *outside* of each "joint" on the straw. This can be tricky, because if you tape the pieces in the wrong position, your fingers won't look right. It's best to attach each cardboard piece while you're bending the straw at the nearest joint. The bent straw makes it easier to see where you should attach the cardboard.

Once all three cardboard "bones" are attached to a straw, test the straw again by pulling down on its tendon. Does the straw curl up and snap back easily? Make sure your cardboard pieces don't overlap each other. And make sure you don't place the tape over the exposed string at the joints!

(Hint: At this point, you may choose to make a few extra fingers, and perhaps a spare thumb, too. You'll get better at making them with practice and testing. Choose the best ones to use. Once you move beyond this step and start assembling your robo-hand, it's a lot harder to go back and fix the straws!)

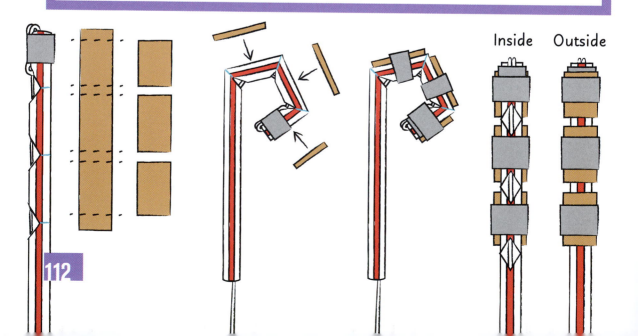

Inside   Outside

Make the **PALM**

Cut a rectangular piece of the thick cardboard roughly the size of your palm. Lay your four finger straws on top of the cardboard. (Save the thumb for later.) Use the outline of the hand you drew in Step 1 as a guide, and duct-tape the bottom sides of the four straws to the cardboard. Cut another piece of thick cardboard the same size and duct-tape it on top of the straws—the bottom of your straws should now be sandwiched securely between two thick pieces of cardboard. You've made a palm!

Now for the back of the hand. Use the outline as a guide and cut another thick piece of cardboard, roughly the size of your hand from the wrist to the bottoms of your fingers. This piece should be larger than the size you used for your palm. Tape your cardboard sandwich, with the fingers securely taped inside, to this larger piece. Your hand is almost done!

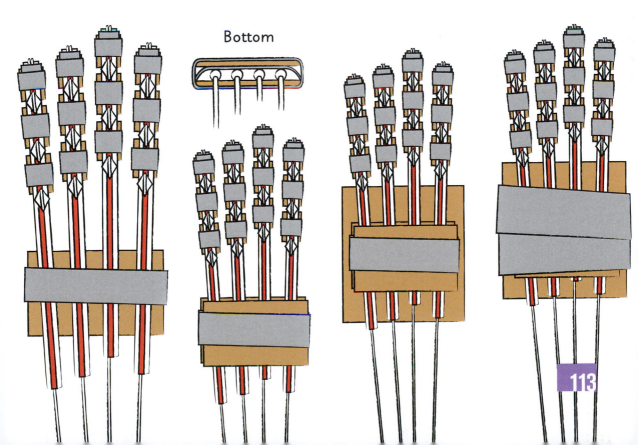

Bottom

Attach the **THUMB**

Humans have *opposable thumbs*. You can twist your thumb around to hold things. Look at how your thumb bends. The thumb itself has joints, but the base is also angled away from the palm. This angle lets your thumb close your hand around objects.

To attach your robo-thumb, first make another "cardboard sandwich," putting one piece of cardboard on the bottom side of the straw, and one piece on the top. Secure with tape. This sandwich should be smaller, since it's only holding one thumb.

Now comes the tricky part. Cut a small strip of thick cardboard and fold it in half. Tape one folded side to the cardboard sandwich holding your thumb. Tape the other folded side to the cardboard back of the hand. This folded cardboard will set the thumb out at an angle from the rest of the fingers. Be sure that the thumb joints are facing inward, towards the other fingers. Use your own thumb as a guide. Once you've got the thumb connected and the joints bend inward, secure the entire palm, hand, and thumb piece with a few more strips of duct tape. And give yourself a hand! No, seriously—you've just made a robo-hand.

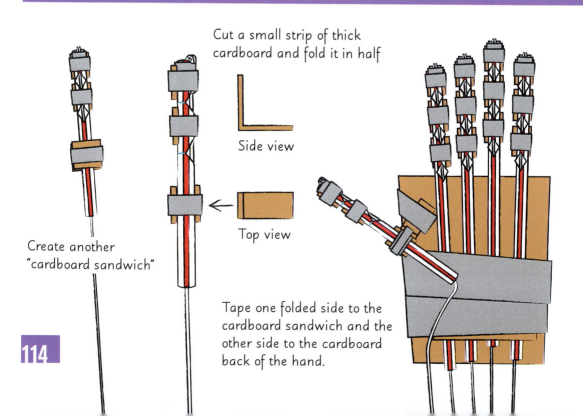

Create another "cardboard sandwich"

Cut a small strip of thick cardboard and fold it in half

Side view

Top view

Tape one folded side to the cardboard sandwich and the other side to the cardboard back of the hand.

Make the **WRIST**

In humans, the hand's tendons connect to muscles in the forearm. Your robot hand should be no different. Cut another rectangle of sturdy cardboard. Duct tape one end of this rectangle to the bottom of your palm. Then tape the other end to the inside of a toilet tissue tube. The tube should fit snugly against the bottom of the hand. Flatten the tube a bit so the straws hanging from the end of the palm can all fit inside of it.

Cut 5 new plastic drinking straws the length of the tube and tape them to the inside of the tube. Pull each string down through the straws inside of the tube. Make sure to keep the strings untangled at this point, and to keep them in their right order, with the pinky on one end and the thumb on the other. This setup will ensure that your strings don't get tangled inside of the wrist.

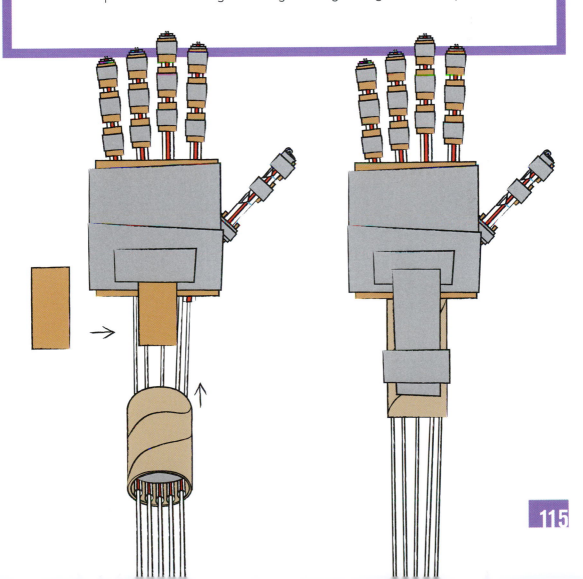

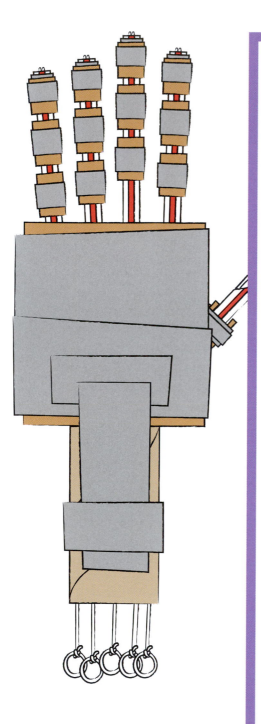

FINISH *the hand*

Once your strings are all sticking out from the bottom of the wrist, tie their ends into loops that fit around your own fingers. (If you have five inexpensive keychain rings to spare for this experiment, you can also tie or tape the strings to them!) Make sure the loops or rings are all relatively even, so you can easily put all of your fingers and thumb through them at once. You might also choose to label each string, according to which finger they control!

Practice moving the robo-hand's fingers with your own finger motions. If your robo-hand's fingers aren't bending right, you can make minor adjustments by enlarging the diamond-shaped cutouts at the joints with scissors. The bigger the holes, the easier the straws will bend.

You can also decorate the hand by drawing circuits and lights or wrapping parts of it in aluminum foil. Just make sure you don't cover up any of the joints—they need to bend freely for the hand to work. And there you have it—you've made yourself a complete robo-hand!

REAL-LIFE ROBOTS:
All Robo-Hands on Deck!

The National Aeronautics and Space Administration—NASA—is developing a robot with some fancy hands. Called the "Robonaut," this automaton's hands are based on human hands. The Robonaut can grasp tiny objects like tweezers, or it can lift heavy loads. NASA expects the robot will prove useful when working outside the International Space Station, because when humans go outside—in outer space—they have to wear bulky space suits and gloves. Because the Robonaut's hands are so similar to a human's, they'll be easy for a human to control, too.

Some of the most impressive robotic "hands" are used in modern surgery. These robotic devices don't actually look much like hands. Expert surgeons control them remotely. The robots have tiny cameras next to their "fingers" that let their human controllers see a close-up view of what's going on. Robotic surgery machines can make much smaller and more precise cuts than a human surgeon could with his or her own hands!

HOMEMADE ICE CREAM

WHEN YOU'RE WALKING down a sidewalk in the cold winter, with the beautiful white snow transformed into a gross brown slush, eating delicious ice cream might not be the first thing on your mind. But actually, ice cream has a lot in common with that slush on the street! Ice cream has a soft, creamy texture for the same reason that slush is, well, slushy. And you can make homemade ice cream the same way that road crews help make slush—with salt and ice.

MATERIALS

- 1 cup kosher salt (or ¾ cup table salt)
- Ice cubes
- 1 large-sized zipper-lock bag
- 1 medium-sized zipper-lock bag
- Mixing bowl
- Empty pillowcase or towel

Note: *Your bags must be freezer-safe and seal completely, otherwise they will leak.*

ICE CREAM INGREDIENTS

- 1 cup milk
- 1 cup half-and-half cream
- ¼ cup maple or chocolate syrup
- 1 teaspoon vanilla extract

More flavors: *Want to make a fruit slushy instead of ice cream? Use 2-3 cups of cold fruit juice or apple cider in place of all of the ice cream ingredients. Follow the same steps to make your treat!*

SALT *your ice*

Fill the large-sized zipper-lock bag most of the way with ice cubes. Pour salt into the bag. Shake the bag for a few minutes until the salt and ice are mixed well and the ice starts to melt. Then put the bag into the freezer for about an hour.

Now take a look at your salty ice cubes. They're even more melted now—even though they've been sitting in the freezer! Why is that? It's the salt working its magic (or to be more accurate, it's chemistry). Salt lowers the freezing point of water, causing this water to melt.

Water, like most things, is made of *molecules*. A molecule is a group of atoms. As water cools, these molecules stop moving around and begin to form solid crystals—ice. Imagine the molecules in an ice cube as building blocks. Want to make more ice? Just stack up a few more water molecules. Easy!

But when you add salt to the mix, things get complicated because now you have to stack up *two* kinds of molecules, and they have different shapes. Imagine building an ice cube not just with regular bricks (water molecules) but also with a few random pyramids or balls (salt) thrown in.

The result is that when you add salt to ice, the ice melts into super-cold water. This is why people sprinkle salt on roads and sidewalks during the icy winter months. The salt causes snow and ice to melt, even when the temperature is below freezing.

Prepare your **ICE CREAM BASE**

Mix together the milk, half-and-half cream, syrup, and vanilla extract in a bowl. This is your ice cream base. Pour the base into the medium-sized bag. Seal the bag tightly, pressing out as much air as you can.

Now take out your big bag of ice, salt, and frigid saltwater. Be careful handling this bag! Have you ever held your fingers under ice water? It hurts, doesn't it? Well, the saltwater in that bag is even colder than ice water, so don't let it touch your skin directly.

Put the smaller bag (the one filled with ice cream base) inside of the larger bag. Carefully—it's cold!—arrange the ice around the smaller bag. Seal the larger bag tightly, with the smaller bag still inside, and shake it a few times to distribute materials evenly.

CHURN *your ice cream*

Now for the fun part! Put the bags—one sealed inside the other—inside of an empty pillowcase. If you don't have a spare pillowcase, you can use a towel and wrap it up tightly.

Then, jiggle and shake the pillowcase for about 10 minutes. Your goal here is to keep the bags in constant motion. This constant jiggling and stirring is called *churning*. It's what gives ice cream and slushies their smooth, creamy texture. (The pillowcase or towel helps protect your hands from the cold.) Take turns churning with a partner if your arms get tired!

Enjoy your TREAT

Have you ever put a liquid—like fruit juice, chocolate milk, or even melted ice cream—into the freezer? The resulting substance might be cold and sweet, and might even taste good, but its texture will be as hard as a solid block of ice. In contrast, your spoon can glide easily through true ice cream. That's because true ice cream is made of lots of very small ice crystals, with sugary liquid and air in between them. Churning keeps these ice crystals small and separate, and it introduces air into the mixture, much like whipping cream or egg whites. But once true ice cream melts into a liquid, there isn't as much air in the mixture, and the liquid re-freezes into a solid state.

The slush you find on the streets is the result of a similar process. Slush is made of lots of very small ice crystals bound together with cold water and a bit of air. People "churn" slush by walking on it, or by driving over it.

After your 10 minutes of churning, the super-cold salt-and-ice should have frozen your ice cream, while the churning action should ensure it's nice and creamy. This activity makes enough ice cream for about three people. Eat it quickly, though! Unlike store-bought ice cream, homemade ice cream quickly becomes icy if you store it in the freezer.

MAKE YOUR OWN SNOWFLAKE

HAVE YOU EVER watched snowflakes fall from the sky? From tiny to large, each snowflake is individually formed high above the ground in the clouds. Snow is made up of thousands of tiny crystals of ice. It may take about 100 snow crystals to clump together to form one snowflake! Each snowflake has its own unique shape and pattern. Snowflakes come in a seemingly endless variety of shapes, but nearly all flakes have six sides. Try this activity to make your own snowflake!

MATERIALS

- Pipe cleaners
- Ruler
- Scissors
- String
- Wide-mouth glass jar
- Tablespoon
- Pure borax
- Boiling water
- Pencil
- Optional: Magnifying glass

What's Borax? Borax is a safe, common household ingredient found in several products such as toothpaste and cleaners. Pure borax can be found in many grocery stores in the laundry detergent aisle. Be sure to follow the safety note listed on each box! If borax is unavailable, you can substitute sugar or salt—the activity might just take a bit longer!

Shape the **FLAKE**

Cut three segments of pipe cleaner into 4-inch (10-centimeter) lengths. (Using a white or light blue pipe cleaner will help the flake look like real snow!) Lay the pipe cleaners over one another so that the points of the flake create a six-sided shape. Twist all three segments together at their centers to attach the branches. You've just formed the structure of your snowflake!

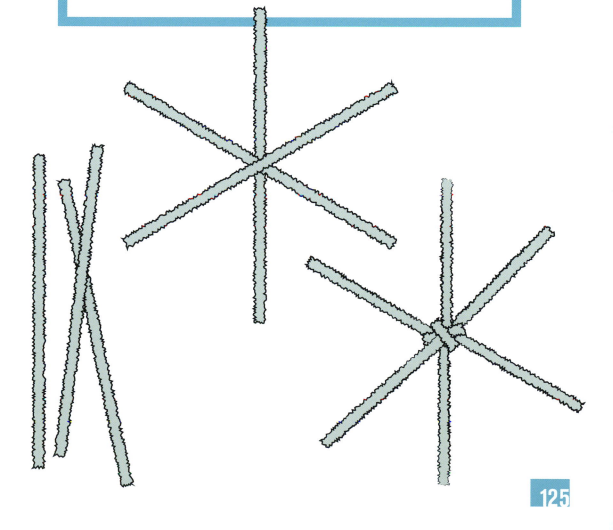

Wind the **STRING**

Starting at the center, tie one end of string to one of the snowflake's branches. Keeping the long portion of the string attached, cut any excess string away from the knot. Wind the piece of string around the branch, moving from the center up to the point, and then wind the string back down to the center again. You should form two rows of string on this one branch. Using the same piece of string, move to the next branch and continue winding the string up the second branch and back down again to the center. Repeat until all of the branches are covered in two rows of string. (Be sure to use the same piece of string to wind the entire flake!) Once all branches are covered in string, tie a final knot around the point of one branch, securing all of the string to the flake. Be sure to leave excess string to form a hanger for the snowflake.

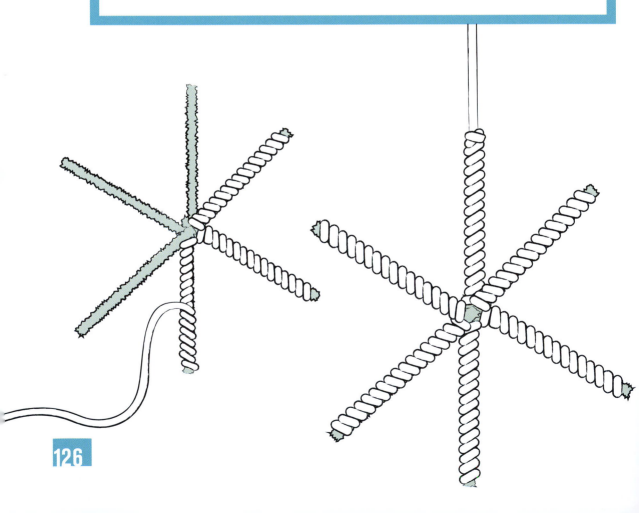

HANG *the flake*

Tie the piece of string attached to the snowflake to the mid-point of a pencil. Knot this spot two or three times. Cut away any excess string from the knot on the pencil. Your snowflake should now be freely hanging off of the pencil. Your pipe cleaner, string, and pencil should be tightly attached together.

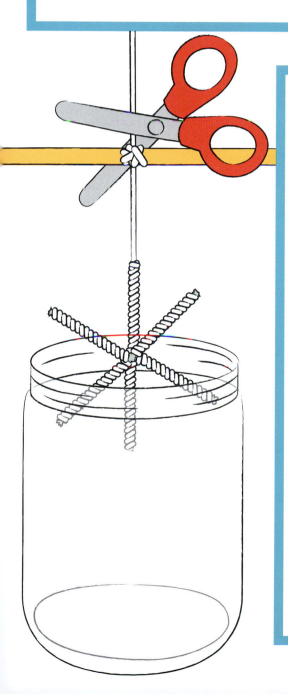

PREPARE *the water*

Selecting the right container is important for forming your snowflake crystals. Test the shape of your glass jar by making sure that the snowflake can easily pass through the opening, without bending. The flake should be able to hang freely in the jar and not touch the jar's sides or bottom. The jar's opening should also allow for the pencil to rest on the top by itself.

Once you've selected the right jar, ask an adult to help you fill the container with boiling water, almost to the top. Mix in about 3 ¼ tablespoons of borax for every 1 cup of water in the container. (If you're using salt or sugar, be sure to add an extra tablespoon per cup of water used!) Carefully stir the borax into the hot water until it is dissolved. Some particles may settle on the bottom of the jar.

SOAK *the flake*

Gently lower the snowflake into the jar, hanging it in the solution. Rest the pencil on mouth of the container. The flake should be completely submerged in the solution and should not be touching the jar's sides or bottom.

Let the snowflake soak for at least eight hours, or even overnight! Check back every three hours to see how the flake changes as it sits in the borax solution. Be careful not to touch the flake or move the pencil during this time—the snowflake needs time to crystalize!

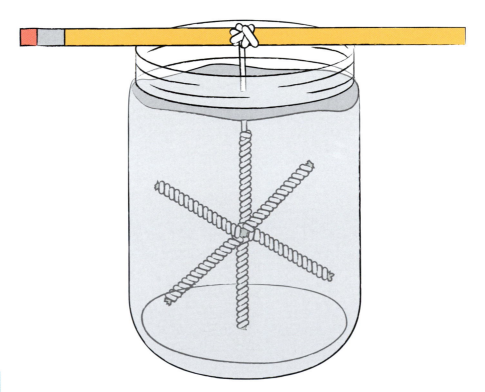

Dry the CRYSTALS

After the flake has soaked, slowly draw the snowflake up from the solution. Hundreds of tiny crystals have formed around the flake! Let the snowflake dry completely—so that the crystals tightly attach to the flake.

Use a magnifying glass to get a closer view of the tiny crystals. Are the crystals all the same size and shape?

Hang the flake near a sunny window to see even more interesting crystal patterns!

Forming Snowflakes

In the clouds, snow begins to form when tiny supercooled water droplets hit a particle of dust in the air and freeze. *Supercooled* means that water is cooled below its usual freezing point without solidifying. As a snow crystal moves through the air, it hits other crystals and water droplets and grows bigger and bigger. Ice crystals fall faster as they grow larger. They may collide with one another to make snowflakes. When a flake is too heavy to stay in the clouds, it floats down to the ground as snow.

Individual snowfalls have many different types and combinations of crystals. Nearly all snow crystals have six sides, but they vary in shape. The crystals are six-sided because the water molecules within them link together in six-sided patterns. There are many kind of patterns like hexagons, six-pointed stars, and familiar crystallized snowflake branches.

PHASES OF THE MOON

THE MOON SEEMS like it's a shapeshifter. One day it looks like a crescent. Another day it looks *gibbous*—fatter than a half circle, skinnier than a full circle. Sometimes you can see the *full moon*, the entire bright circle of the thing. And other times—during the *new moon*—you can't really see the moon in the sky at all. These different shapes are called the *phases of the moon*.

The moon does not give off light itself. We see the moon because the sun shines on it, and the moon reflects the sun's light. And in fact, the moon doesn't change shape at all. All that changes is how much of the sunlit side of the moon we can see from Earth. The reason the moon goes through phases is simple: the moon *orbits* (revolves) around Earth about once each month. In this activity, you'll see exactly how the moon's orbit causes its phases.

MATERIALS

- Flashlight
- Volleyball or other light-colored ball
- Camera

SET UP *your sun, Earth, and moon*

Find the darkest room in your home, ideally a room without windows, such as a bathroom or a basement room. Put the flashlight on one side of the room and turn it on. This flashlight is going to play the role of the sun.

Clear a space on the floor, across from the flashlight. Put the volleyball and camera down next to each other. The volleyball is the moon. The camera is Earth—or rather, someone on the surface of Earth, looking up at the moon.

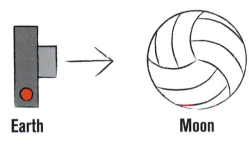

Earth   **Moon**

Sun

Robots on the Moon!

Humans like to pat themselves on the back for landing on the moon: "One small step for man, one giant leap for mankind," in the words of Neil Armstrong. But robots have been to the moon, too! Yutu, a Chinese robot, became the most recent robot to visit the moon, in 2013. Yutu, which means "Jade Rabbit" in Chinese, is a rover specially made to move across the harsh, dusty lunar surface. Humans can control Yutu remotely from Earth.

PHOTOGRAPH *the moon*

Turn off the lights in the room, so the flashlight is the only source of illumination. Carefully make your way back to the volleyball and camera.

Now take a photograph of the volleyball. If necessary, move the volleyball closer or farther away from the camera, so it shows up well in the shot. How much of the volleyball is illuminated?

Move the volleyball in an "orbit" (circle) around the camera. (The real moon orbits Earth in a counterclockwise direction.) Take seven more pictures as you move the ball into new positions. You'll need to swivel the camera around the same spot to keep the ball in the shot—but don't actually move the camera to a different place on the floor. Only the volleyball should change position. When you find yourself in between the flashlight and the volleyball, try to position the ball so that your shadow doesn't fall on it.

You see

Waxing half

Match the photos TO PHASES

Look at the photos you've taken. Do they look familiar? The volleyball's appearance in the photos should change, just like the phases of the moon. When the ball is between the camera and the flashlight, it hardly shows up in pictures. This is called the *new moon*. As the ball circles around, more of its lit-up surface becomes visible in the photos—first as a crescent, then as a half-moon, then a *gibbous* moon, and finally, a full moon. As the moon "grows" in apparent size, from new to full, it is said to be *waxing*.

As the moon continues circling from its full-moon phase, it is then said to be *waning*, or shrinking. It goes through the same stages in reverse—gibbous, half, crescent, and then back to the new moon. If you've taken eight pictures, you should have a picture of each phase of the moon—(1) new, (2) waxing crescent, (3) waxing half, (4) waxing gibbous, (5) full, (6) waning gibbous, (7) waning half, and (8) waning crescent.

So you see—the moon itself doesn't change during its phases. Only its appearance does, from the perspective of us earthlings.

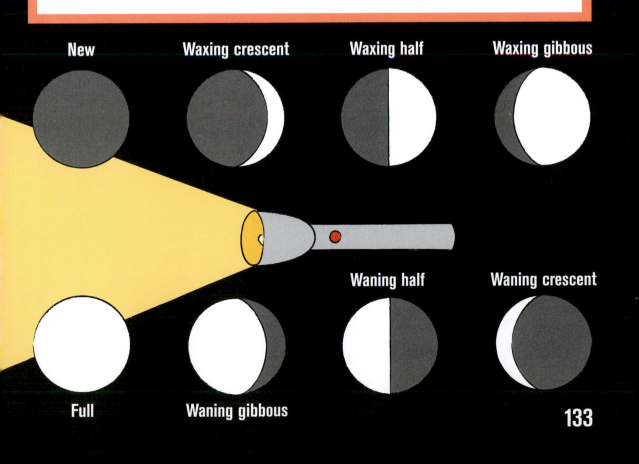

New   Waxing crescent   Waxing half   Waxing gibbous

Waning half   Waning crescent

Full   Waning gibbous

SOLAR SYSTEM MOBILE

THE *SOLAR SYSTEM* is the name for the sun and all the things that orbit (revolve) around it. This system has eight planets altogether. The *inner planets* are four small, rocky worlds—Mercury, Venus, Earth (that's us!), and Mars. The four *outer planets* are Jupiter, Saturn, Uranus, and Neptune. The outer planets are huge and made mostly of gas, so they're sometimes called *gas giants*.

Even though the solar system is just one of billions and billions and billions of star systems, it's still pretty huge. For example, Earth is about 93 million miles (150 kilometers) from the sun at the center of the solar system. If you were to somehow drive a car at highway speed from your house to the sun, it would take about 175 years! And Earth is pretty close to the sun, all things considered—that's why it gets so nice and toasty here during the summer. Neptune, the outermost planet in the solar system, is about 2.8 trillion miles (4.5 trillion kilometers) away from the sun.

There's no good way to make an accurate model of the solar system that accounts for the vastness of space between the sun and planets. In a true scale model of the solar system—one that fits on a table, at least—the planets would have to be so small that you'd need a microscope to see them. Instead, we're going to make a model that's a little less accurate but still shows all eight of the planets, in all their wonder. It even divides the inner planets from the outer planets. Not bad!

MATERIALS

- 4 dowel rods:
  one 17 inches (43 centimeters)
  one 21 inches (53 centimeters)
  one 35 inches (89 centimeters)
  one 43 inches (109 centimeters)
- Spool of clear nylon thread or fishing line
- 4 plastic or metal rings, 3/4 inch (2 centimeters) across
- Large piece of white poster board
- Geometric compass
- Scissors
- Glue
- Crayons or markers
- Tape
- Hole punch
- Yardstick or measuring tape
- Large paper plate
- Small hook for hanging the mobile

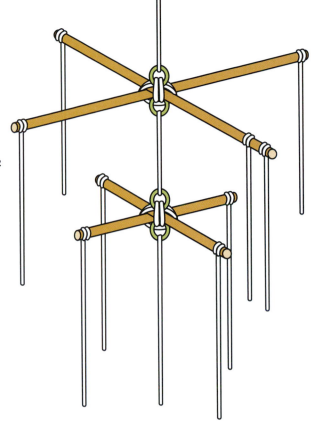

Make your HANGERS

Cross the two longer dowel rods so one end of each rod sticks out 1 inch (2.5 centimeters) farther than the other end, as shown in the illustrations. Tie them together with nylon thread. Do the same with the two shorter rods. Tie a ring above and below each pair of rods at the points where the rods cross.

Cut an 8-inch (20-centimeter) piece of nylon thread. Tie one end of the thread to the ring below the longer rods. Tie the other end to the ring on top of the shorter rods. Leave 6 inches (15 centimeters) of thread between the rings.

Cut nine 16-inch (41-centimeter) pieces of thread. These will be the threads from which your planets and sun will hang. Tie eight to the ends of each rod, and tie the last one from the central, bottom ring.

Finally, cut a long thread from which to hang the entire mobile. Tie this to the topmost ring.

CUT OUT *the sun and planets*

To make the planets and the sun, draw nine circles on the poster board using a geometric compass. Set your compass to the radii (distances from the center) shown in the chart below. Ask an adult to help you if you don't know how to use a compass.

Sun: 4 1/2 inches (11.5 centimeters)

Jupiter: 3 3/4 inches (9.5 centimeters)

Saturn: 3 1/4 inches (8.5 centimeters), plus rings

Neptune: 2 1/2 inches (6.5 centimeters)

Uranus: 2 1/4 inches (6 centimeters)

Earth: 1 1/2 inches (4 centimeters)

Venus: 1 1/2 inches (4 centimeters)

Mars: 1 1/8 inches (3 centimeters)

Mercury: 1 inch (2.5 centimeters)

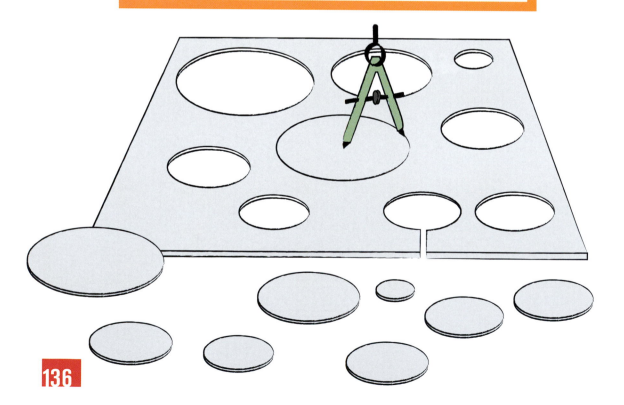

COLOR *your planets and sun*

Use crayons or markers to color your cut-outs. Use the pictures in this activity for reference, or look up pictures of the planets yourself. Don't forget all the cool details, like Earth's continents and the Great Red Spot on Jupiter.

Now, Saturn is a planet that's famous for its rings. (Actually, all the gas giants have rings, but the others' are pretty faint.) Use the paper plate for Saturn's rings. Color just the outer edge of the plate, as shown in the illustration. Cut a slit about 3 3/4 inches (9.5 centimeters) long in the middle of the plate. Slip the Saturn model through the slit and tape it in place.

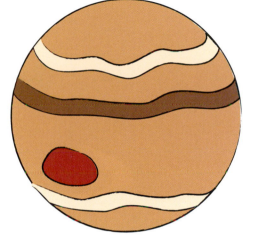

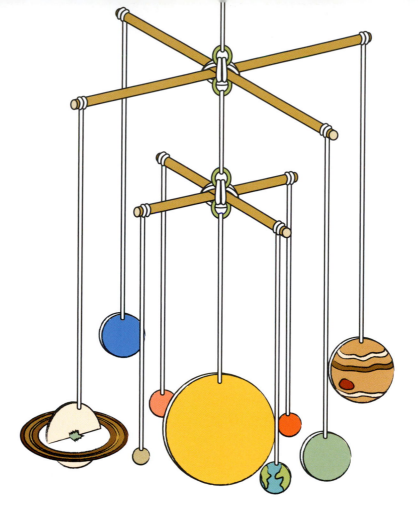

ATTACH *everything together*

Punch a hole near the top of your sun and each planet. Tie your sun and planets to the mobile, as shown in the illustration. Mercury, the planet closest to the sun, should hang from the shortest section of rod, Venus from the next shortest section, and so on, in each planet's order from the sun. Uranus and Neptune should hang from the longest rod. Look at the picture of the finished mobile for help. Now you can hang the solar system anywhere you like!

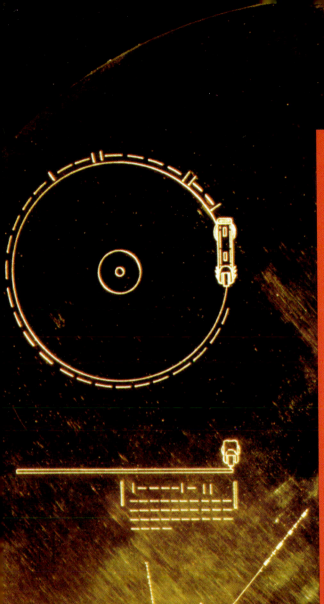

The Farthest Journey

In 1977, humans from the United States launched two robots to the farthest reaches of the solar system—a pair of space probes, Voyager 1 and Voyager 2. These probes passed beyond the orbits of Jupiter, Saturn, Uranus, and Neptune. They're currently flying out into the space beyond the planets.

These robots mark the farthest any presences from the planet Earth have ever traveled. Scientists attached "golden records" to the two spacecraft. The records are actual phonograph records. Natural sounds and music from Earth are encoded on the records' grooves. The back of the records have engraved pictures that show diagrams from physics, as well as the location of Earth—on the off chance that any intelligent aliens find the Voyagers.

In 2013, scientists confirmed that Voyager 1 crossed a region of space called the *heliopause*. The heliopause is the edge of a vast "bubble" created by the sun's magnetic field.

AXEL'S INTERNAL PRESSURE

"Well, that wasn't exactly a mental break, but I couldn't help learning more about the solar system. I saw that mobile hanging from the ceiling when I walked into Grandfather's laboratory and just had to find out more about our planetary neighbors! And the ice cream I made was tasty, too!" Mollie said as she pet Feline.

Axel walked over to Mollie and picked up her solar system mobile.

"A good use of knowledge, Mollie. Well ... BEEP... done ... BEEP BLOOP BLORP..." Axel started to mumble. His eyes started to blink quickly and his buttons lit up!

"Axel, what's wrong? Oh no! It looks like all of the robot reboots and activations I've made today have caused too much pressure to build up inside your chest and head."

Mollie looked to the manual. "There's no section on this! Let me think. I remember learning about air pressure when I was reading through Grandfather's Experimental Log. It was the Balloon in a Bottle activity. It said that when air pressure builds up, one way to relieve that pressure is by letting some air out of a small hole."

Mollie stopped to look at Axel, wondering how she could get some air out. "I know! If I open the latch to the top of his head just a little bit, some of the air will leak out, and the air pressure will return to normal. If I use a bit of modeling clay to keep the latch open, Axel can continue to move around and communicate without having this problem again!"

141

BALLOON IN A BOTTLE

SOMETIMES at the end of a long day of school, or perhaps late at night when you're studying for a test, it may feel like you just can't cram any more information into your head. There's too much stuff already swimming around inside of your skull for you to remember a former vice president's name, or that the Pythagorean Theorem has to do with triangles and not pythons.

Now, human heads aren't full of air, and our brains aren't balloons. But it is hard, in general, to stuff something into a container that's already full. In this activity, you'll explore the idea of air pressure by learning how to blow up a balloon inside of an empty bottle.

MATERIALS

- Large, clear plastic soft-drink bottle, with screw-top lid
- Balloon
- Water
- Nail or other sharp object (for poking a hole in the bottle)

Caution!

Make sure an adult is present to help you use sharp tools carefully.

142

Try to INFLATE

Make sure your bottle is empty. Place the balloon into the bottle, stretching the open end of the balloon snugly over the bottle's opening. Now try to blow up the balloon so it inflates inside of the bottle.

Seems like it should be easy, right? Well, don't try too hard—you might faint! It turns out that it's impossible to blow up a balloon inside an empty bottle. It's impossible because, in fact, the bottle is not really empty! There's air in there. Air, like other fluids, has *pressure*. When you push against air, the air pushes back.

Normally, when you blow up a balloon, all you're doing is forcing air into a stretchy balloon—which isn't that hard. But when the balloon is inside of a rigid container, blowing it up also means pushing and squeezing the air that's already inside of the container, to make room for the expanding balloon. You either need superhuman lung power, or you need to give the air inside the bottle some means of escape.

Make an ESCAPE ROUTE

Take the balloon out of the bottle and fill the bottle up with water. Put the cap on. Ask an adult to help you use the nail to poke a hole in the bottle, near the bottom. Once you pierce a hole, unscrew the cap and empty out the water. (The water makes it easier to poke a hole!)

Place the balloon back into the bottle, stretching the open end of the balloon over the bottle's opening. Now try to blow up the balloon inside the bottle again. Did it inflate?

Not so hard this time, right? By poking a hole in the bottle, you've given the air trapped inside of the bottle a way to escape and make room for the expanding balloon. Remember, air doesn't like getting pressured or squeezed! If air goes into a container, air must go out. So, as you blow air into the balloon and it inflates, this pressure causes the air inside of the bottle to slowly escape through the hole.

Balloon **MAGIC**

Blow up the balloon inside of the bottle again. Now, when the balloon is inflated, hold your finger over the hole you made in the bottle. Then take the balloon away from your mouth.

As long as you hold your finger over the hole, the balloon should stay inflated inside of the bottle—even though the end of the balloon is stretched wide open!

Why does this happen? Well, you know that if you want to put air into a container, you have to let air out of the container to make room. Air doesn't like getting squeezed. But it turns out that the opposite is true, too! Air doesn't like *expanding* to fill a space either. Air likes to stay at a constant pressure. For instance, if the balloon deflated in the sealed bottle, the air inside the bottle would have to expand to fill the extra space— and it doesn't like to do that. So, the air's pressure "pulls" on the balloon, forcing it to stay blown-up—at least, as long as you hold your finger over the hole in the bottle.

EXPERIMENT *further*

Try making a water balloon inside of the bottle. (Make sure you do this outside or at least over a big sink—you're going to splash.) Both air and water are fluids. Neither likes being pressured into smaller spaces. What happens if you inflate the balloon inside of the bottle, fill it with water, and then take your finger off of the hole? What about filling the balloon halfway with water? What happens if you put the lid on? Continue experimenting with the air pressure in your balloon in a bottle to find out!

REAL-LIFE ROBOTS: Robots Under Pressure

If you think poor Axel had a pressure problem, imagine what robots on other planets have to deal with! Other planets have air, too—some more than others. On Venus, the air pressure is 90 times greater than Earth's. The air is so thick and heavy that it can crush metal! But that didn't stop a few brave robots from exploring the surface of Venus. In 1975, a robot named Venera 9 plunged through Venus's thick air, landed on the surface, and started taking pictures—these were the first photographs ever taken from the surface of another planet!

Mars has air, too—but it's much thinner than the air on Earth. The thin air makes it hard for robots to land on Mars because parachutes don't work so well! But a few robots still managed to get there, too. Curiosity, seen below, is the latest robot to land on Mars, in 2012. Because it was so heavy, parachutes weren't enough to slow its fall through Mars' thin air. It had to blast rockets right before it landed to slow down.

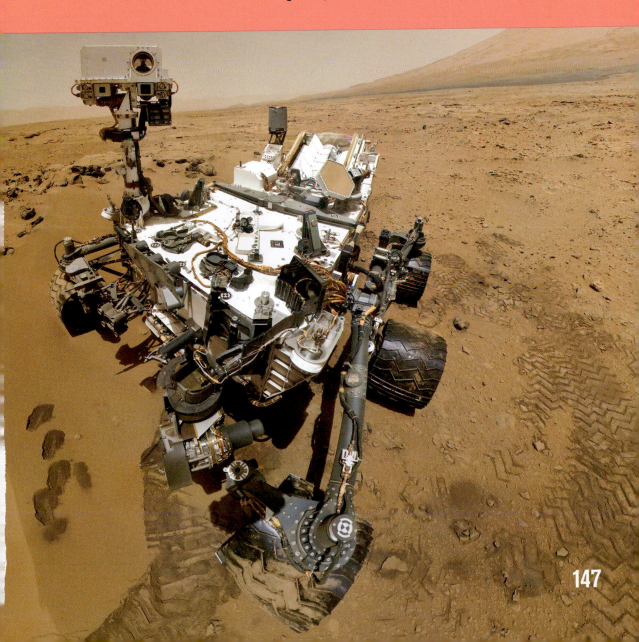

MOLDING MODELING CLAY

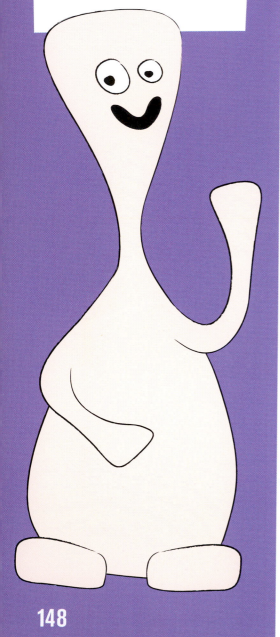

HAVE YOU ever wondered how artists make sculptures, or how designers shape cars, or how craftsmen make jewelry? They all use modeling clay! Using clay allows many skilled people to make a model of the work they are about to create. The clay lets them mold and shape, and re-mold and re-shape until their design is perfect. Then, they use materials, like marble, aluminum, or gold to make the final product! Scientists can also use modeling clay to visually show how molecules bind together, or design a space shuttle, or even model a robot invention!

Sounds simple, right? It is! You can make your own modeling clay with just a few simple ingredients. This recipe makes about a cup of modeling clay. (If you need more, you can double the recipe!) You can make models of anything you choose—from a small city to your own pet! Don't forget to use food coloring or glitter to make each batch unique!

MATERIALS

- Large bowl
- Measuring cups and spoons
- Spoon
- 1 ¼ cups flour
- ⅓ cup salt
- ½ cup water
- 2 teaspoons vegetable oil
- Food coloring or glitter (optional)
- Airtight container (optional)

MIX *the dry materials*

Measure the flour and the salt and pour them into a large bowl. (Remember to increase the amounts, if you're doubling the recipe!) Stir the ingredients until they are well mixed together. These dry materials will act as the base for your modeling clay.

STIR IN *the wet materials*

Using a measuring cup, portion the water and pour it into the bowl with the dry materials. Then, measure the vegetable oil and empty it into the bowl. Use a spoon to stir the wet materials into the dry ones. Continue stirring for about 30 seconds, or until the materials form a sticky type of dough. (Hint: If the dough seems too watery, you can add a little more flour to make just the right consistency.) Be careful not to over mix!

Stirring helps a chemical reaction take place between the water and the flour. Chemicals in the flour form a rubbery substance called *gluten*. This gluten makes your dough nice and stretchy. Amazing!

KNEAD *the clay*

Once the clay dough has just come together, take it out of the bowl and *knead* it with your hands. Push and pull the dough with your fingers. If the dough sticks to your fingers too much, you can put a dusting of flour on your hands and continue kneading. Work the clay for about a minute until it is smooth.

Kneading together water and flour is the same process that bakers use to make bread dough! They combine ingredients like flour, eggs, and yeast to make a sticky dough that bakes into bread— they just use a lot less salt!

STEP 4

Add **COLOR**

After the dough is smooth, flatten it out on your palm. Carefully, add a few drops of food coloring or a sprinkle of glitter directly onto the clay. Work the color or glitter into the clay with your fingers, kneading the clay a few more times. As you knead, the color or glitter should stick to the clay and spread evenly throughout.

Your batch of modeling clay is finished! Have fun forming models of any object you choose. When you're finished, store the clay in an airtight container so that you can play with it again and again!

151

AXEL'S MEMORY

"Is that better, Axel?" Mollie reached to the top of Axel's head and adjusted the latch. She propped it open with a bit of sticky putty she found on the shelf. Axel's head was now partially open, allowing some air to escape.

As air flowed out from the top, Axel's eyes stopped their blinking and the button lights went off. "Hello, Mollie!" Axel said. "Thank you. My internal pressure is restored to normal."

"Oh, Axel! I am so glad that you are talking again. It is such a relief that I kept my grandfather's invention alive, don't you think, Feline? Phew!"

Mollie went to the instruction manual.

Memory

To unlock the essential memory component of this robot, the internal components must be strategically balanced. Powering Axel allows for sight, speech, and movement. Beware: Such mechanics cause pressure buildup and bodily equilibrium must be achieved.

"Pressure! Of course, Grandfather knew about this. But, I remembered what I knew about air pressure and applied it to helping Axel. Now that's using my head!"

Once pressure is correctly established, Axel has infinite ability to learn and remember facts and figures—from memorizing the numbers in Pi to assembling an apple pie. This invaluable ability must be carefully monitored. Too much information causes malfunction, and too little stimulation causes shut down. Curious and resourceful scientists will recognize that one day, intelligent robots like this will roam about with the rest of us.

In closing, let Axel forever be remembered as my greatest achievement.

-Doc U. Ment

Mollie looked at Axel with a smile. "Grandfather was right. There are thousands of robots in the world today, but there's only one of you, Axel. I'm glad that I could follow in Grandfather's footsteps to reboot your mechanics! And look at all of the new science knowledge I gained! I learned about so many new science concepts all in one day."

"Affirmative, Mollie. Much knowledge has been acquired today. What should we work on next?"

153

"This is going to be so much fun to work with a real robot!" Mollie said with excitement.

"Mollie. Look at this." Axel drew back a curtain hanging on the far wall. Feline dashed into the room behind it and leaped up on a high shelf.

"What did you find, Axel? These look like more inventions—I don't even recognize some of these objects. And since this is Grandfather's lab, I bet he was working on these, too!"

"When I access my memory storage, I can remember Doc assembling me. My memory circuits contain data about other inventions he worked on as well," Axel said.

"You can remember information from that long ago?" Mollie gasped as she inspected the other inventions. "Amazing! Do you remember anything else about these gadgets?"

"Affirmative, Mollie. My memory circuits stored the words spoken by your grandfather! He said, 'A scientist's skills must always be in use. Fiddling with one invention is a pastime. Developing a collection is an occupation.'"

"What a great motto—a scientist's work is never done! Brilliant! There is always something new to learn. If I can repair Axel, I can try to work on Grandfather's other inventions, too! I know he would be so proud."

"Affirmative, Mollie. And I can help you."

"Alright, Axel! That sounds like a fantastic plan. We begin tomorrow!"

MEASURING EQUIVALENTS

1 gallon
4 quarts
8 pints
16 cups
3.8 liters

1 quart
2 pints
4 cups
32 ounces
0.95 liters

1 tablespoon
3 teaspoons
½ fluid ounce
15 milliliters

1 pint
2 cups
16 ounces
480 milliliters

1 cup
8 ounces
240 milliliters

¼ cup
4 tablespoons
12 teaspoons
2 ounces
60 milliliters

ACKNOWLEDGMENTS

All illustrations by Matt Carrington, World Book, Inc.
The publishers would like to thank the following sources
for the use of their photographs in this book:

16	© Shutterstock
25	NASA
29	© Shutterstock
41	© Shutterstock
51	Gordan Ugarkovic, NASA/JPL/SSI; ESA
89	© Shutterstock
99	© Shutterstock
103	© Shutterstock
117	NASA
123	© FoodCollection/Superstock
139	NASA
147	NASA/JPL–Caltech/Malin Space Science Systems

NOTES